Publications of the California Historical Survey Commission

Edited by
Owen C. Coy, Ph.D.
Director of the Commission

THE ARCHITECTURAL HISTORY

OF

Mission San Carlos Borromeo

CALIFORNIA

BY

Frances Rand Smith

Published by the

California Historical Survey Commission

BERKELEY, 1921

CALIFORNIA STATE PRINTING OFFICE
SACRAMENTO, 1921

FRONTISPIECE. *Ruins of San Carlos about 1865.*

This photo by Johnson is the earliest photograph at hand. This is seen by the remains of the wall against the facade of the church, the condition of the roof over the chapel, and the ruins in the rear to the left.

LETTER OF TRANSMITTAL.

To His Excellency, WILLIAM D. STEPHENS, *Governor,*
Sacramento, California.

SIR: Herewith is presented *The Architectural History of Mission San Carlos Borromeo,* the first of a projected series dealing with the architectural history of the Spanish missions of California, the work being undertaken under the statutes prescribing the duties of the Commission.

Respectfully submitted.

CALIFORNIA HISTORICAL SURVEY COMMISSION,

JOHN F. DAVIS, *Chairman,*
HERBERT E. BOLTON,
EDWARD A. DICKSON,
OWEN C. COY, *Director.*

Berkeley, California, August 15, 1921.

2—11308

EDITOR'S PREFACE

This volume is the first of a projected series relating to the architectural history of the Spanish missions of California. The work was undertaken by the Historical Survey Commission under a statute of 1917 (Statutes, 1917, Chap. 410), defining its duties to be among other things "to investigate and acquire information as to the physical characteristics of the several missions which were maintained in the State of California under the charge of the Franciscan fathers."

For many years Mrs. Frances Rand Smith of Palo Alto had been engaged in the study of the old California missions and she already had copious notes, sketches, photographs and models of several of the missions. The commission therefore sought her cooperation in this work and during the summer of 1918 obtained from her the manuscript, sketches and photographs which form the basis for this report. Since that time the author and the commission have been busily engaged in revising, elaborating, and perfecting the original manuscript.

In accordance with the terms of the act a public hearing was held at Carmel, October 31, 1918, at which time the details of this report were carefully gone over by the many persons assembled who represented the Church, historical and landmarks societies, and many others. Many interesting points were developed but no material additions to the information or adverse criticism of the findings of the commission were offered.

Subsequent excavations carried on by Father Raymond M. Mestres, in charge of the parish in which San Carlos Mission is located, brought to light much valuable data and a wealth of detail regarding the mission buildings. These excavations together with continued historical research and the gathering of additional photographs has made it possible for the commission to supplement materially the original text.

In a work of this character, where the official historical records and the archeological remains are not complete but must be supplemented by other less reliable data, it is necessary to keep clearly in mind the varying degrees of reliability of the evidence presented. At least three classes of information have been used in this work. First, the archeological remains as seen in the buildings and ruins now extant. In so far as these remains can be identified as parts of the mission before the time of secularization they are the most valuable data to be obtained as to form, material, and dimension. Second, there are the written records. These vary in reliability from the official contemporary records of the padres and the detailed descriptions of more or less accurate observations of scientific explorers, as Lapérouse, Vancouver, Du Petit-Thouars and others, to the less definite and unreliable accounts. Third, the pictorial representations of the missions as shown by sketches, survey-plats, and photographs. The reliability of these last classes increases in the order named. For San Carlos three sketches made by foreign voyagers antedate the time of the photographs: one by Sykes, made about 1794; one by Wm. Smythe, probably made in 1823; and the other published by Laplace in the account of his voyage along the California coast in 1839. They all possess great value but are merely the artist's description, their accuracy depending directly upon the degree of faithfulness with which he represented the scene before him. It is probable that in some cases merely rude pencil sketches were the only definite record made upon the spot, much of the detail being added during the many leisure hours upon shipboard. It is therefore not remarkable that many points may be found in these sketches which cause difficulty in interpretation. The photographs, which first appear during the sixties, are free from this criticism and preserve for us most valuable information of what still remained of these old landmarks. Of particular value are the views of Johnson, Muybridge, Perkins, Watkins and Fiske.

For aid in the prosecution of this work the commission wishes to express its appreciation to His Grace the Most Reverend Edward J. Hanna, Archbishop of San Francisco, and the Right Reverend J. J. Cantwell, Bishop of Monterey and Los Angeles, for their cordial support and assistance; to Monsignor Joseph M. Gleason of Palo Alto; to Reverend Thomas L. O'Neill of Berkeley, who kindly gave much assistance and valuable advice; and especially does it appreciate the help of Father Raymond M. Mestres of Monterey, whose excavations have enabled the commission to incorporate into this report much valuable material which otherwise would have been inaccessible. Gratitude is due the authorities in charge of the Bancroft Collection for the data contained in the valuable transcripts made by Bancroft from the original archives, many of which have subsequently been destroyed. Mr. C. B. Turrill has furnished copies for several excellent illustrations. From the State Library through Miss Eudora Garroutte and Mr. H. C. Peterson many valuable photographs have been obtained, especially those taken by C. W. J. Johnson, now belonging to the Frances M. Hilby Collection of the State Library. From Mrs. Ivy Perkins Cercle of San Francisco were obtained the views taken by her father, Mr. Perkins, the original negatives subsequently having been placed in the State Library. Valuable criticism and advice regarding architectural features were obtained from Mr. Bernard Maybeck and the School of Architecture of the University of California. Mr. B. S. Hayne assisted in observations at the mission and worked into form for reproduction many of the illustrations contained in this report. It scarcely need be added that all students of the California missions are constantly indebted to Father Zephyrin Engelhardt for his scholarly works.

Much historical data has purposely been eliminated because this study is limited closely to the "physical characteristics" of the mission. On the other hand the architectural study might have been made more elaborate in detail had our resources been less limited. If this data is incomplete in some particular it is believed to be all that may be incorporated with a satisfactory historical basis at present. In view of the fact that the greatest number of readers will be neither technically trained historians nor architects an endeavor has been made to avoid an undue amount of technical language or detail in either field.

The actual restoration of these mission structures is not within the province of this commission. What is here presented is set forth in the hope that it may be of assistance to those so engaged, and with the feeling that it will furnish much useful data to that larger group of general readers interested in studying California mission architecture.

OWEN C. COY.

Berkeley, California, June 15, 1921.

AUTHOR'S PREFACE

For assistance in the prosecution and completion of the present work the writer's thanks are due especially to Professor Herbert E. Bolton, for his personal aid and encouragement; to Dr. Owen C. Coy, for his skillful assistance in investigations at the mission and his unfailing guidance in bibliographic studies and preparation of the text; to the Reverend Monsignor Joseph Gleason, for generous contributions from his library and store of personal knowledge of mission history; to Mr. Chas. B. Turrill, for his contribution of many pictures of historical value; to Mr. L. S. Slevin, for the use of his collections of old pictures and his zeal in securing new ones. The cordial aid of these and many other friends has lightened the labor which has lasted through the years since 1908, when this study was begun. The writer hopes that it may be a modest tribute to the achievements of the pious padres who founded our earliest settlements.

FRANCES RAND SMITH.

TABLE OF CONTENTS

LIST OF ILLUSTRATIONS

HISTORICAL NARRATIVE

HISTORICAL NARRATIVE

Mission San Carlos Borromeo was founded on June 3, 1770, by Father Junípero Serra. The first site was on the shore of Monterey Bay, near the spot where Vizcaíno landed, and where the Carmelite friars said mass "in the shadow of a large oak tree, some of whose branches reached the water." Portolá, who had explored the site the previous year, took formal possession of the port on the date mentioned and was present at the founding of the mission. The historic ceremony is described by Father Serra in a contemporary letter as follows:[1]

"On the holy day of Pentecost, the 3rd of June, after having gathered together all the officers of sea and land and all the rest of the people by the side of the little ravine and oak where the Fathers of that other expedition [Vizcaíno] had held their celebration, an altar was erected, the bells were hung up and rung, the hymn *Veni Creator* was sung and the water blessed, and finally a large cross was erected and the royal standard set up. I then sang the first Mass which we suppose has been celebrated here since that long ago, and then we sang the *Hail to Our Lady* before the image of our Most Illustrious Queen which occupied the altar. After that I preached a sermon to the assembled people. After the service had been concluded with the *Te Deum* the officers performed the ceremony of taking formal possession of the land in the name of the King, our lord (whom may God keep). We afterwards ate our dinner together under a shade on the beach. The whole service had been accompanied with much thunder of powder both on land and from the ship. To God alone be given all the honor and glory."

Father Crespi, who was associated with Serra in the administration of the mission, described its founding in the following words:[2]

"On the same day of Pentecost, June 3rd, . . . the Rev. Fr. Presidente of the missions, Fr. Junípero Serra, in the name of the king and of the Rev. Fr. Guardian and the venerable Discretory of the Apostolic College of the Propagation of the Faith, of San Fernando de Mexico, established the new mission under the title of San Carlos Borromeo. Naming as principal patron of the new church the most holy Patriarch St. Joseph, he took possession of it in the name of the said college, and assigned as his fellow missionary Fr. Juan Crespi, his disciple in philosophy."

Temporary buildings were erected for the presidio. An enclosure made of branches and trees and provided with an altar served temporarily as a church. Soon a small chapel was built, together with the living quarters for the padres and the necessary workshops. All was surrounded by a stockade.[3]

The Question of a New Site. Soon after the founding of the mission Father Serra became dissatisfied with its location. He therefore petitioned the proper authorities to be permitted to remove the mission from the site on Monterey Bay to the valley of the Carmel River about a league distant

---

[1]Palou, *Relacion historica de la vida y apostolicas tareas del venerable padre Fray Junípero Serra* (1787 ed.), 101-102. Hereafter cited as *"Vida."* For translation see James edition, p. 98. See also Engelhardt. *The Missions and Missionaries of California,* II, 74-75. for translation from Crespi's account in Palou, *Noticias de la Neuva California* (San Francisco, 1874), II, 268-269.

[2]Engelhardt, II, 77, 78.

[3]Palou, *Noticias,* II, 271-272; *Vida,* 103.

across the peninsula. As the reason for this request he explained that there was but little arable land in the vicinity of the port and that running water for purposes of irrigation was entirely lacking. Another reason doubtless strong in the mind of Father Serra was to provide a greater distance between the mission Indians and the soldiers of the presidio.[4] The proposed location held all of these advantages over the one already selected, for the valley possessed much fertile land for cultivation and the river could furnish all the water needed for irrigation.

Removal to Carmel Valley, 1771. In response to the petition of Fr. Serra, the Viceroy granted the permit to remove the mission to the Carmel River at such place as Serra might select,[5] and also as a personal donation sent a set of vestments consisting of chasuble and dalmaties, which were to be used on solemn occasions.[6] In June, as soon as the order had been received from the Viceroy granting permission for the removal, Serra set out for Carmel Valley to select the site and make ready for the removal of the mission. Leaving at that place several Lower California Indians under the charge of three marines and five soldiers to cut and prepare timbers, Serra hastened to found a mission later known as San Antonio de Padua.[7] Returning to Carmel Valley he found the work progressing too slowly to suit his desires, so he took up his abode at the new mission site on the first of August, 1771. Since the Indians and soldiers had already provided an amount of wood and timbers, Father Serra set about the construction of the necessary buildings, he himself acting as "engineer and overseer." His first work was to have hewn out a great cross, which after being consecrated was raised and fixed in the ground about the center of the area determined for the mission. Near at hand stood a hut in which he lived and another which served provisionally as a church.[8]

Palou gives the following more detailed account of the removal of the Mission:[9]

"As soon as the Mission of San Antonio had been founded, the reverend padre proceeded to the Royal Presidio of Monterey, and although he eagerly desired to go, and found another mission, San Luis Obispo, it was not possible on account of a lack of soldiers for a guard, and so he assisted in removing the mission as His Excellency had ordered; for this purpose it was arranged that Fray Juan Crespi and the ministers destined for San Luis should remain in the Royal Presidio, and the reverend padre determined to proceed to the place on the Carmel, which had been designated, to plan

[4]Palou, *Noticias,* II, 286; Engelhardt, *Missions and Missionaries,* II, 81; Bancroft, *History of California,* **I, 177.**

[5]De Croix to Fages, Nov. 12, 1770, in *Archives of California, Provincial State Papers,* I, 70 (Bancroft Collection, ms.)

[6]Engelhardt, II, 84.

[7]*Ibid,* II, 87; Bancroft, I, 177, based on Palou, *Vida,* 121; (James ed.), 115-116; Palou, *Noticias,* II, 289. This was the first use of these extensive forests for construction purposes of which there is at hand any record.

[8]Palou, *Vida,* 128; (James ed.), 124. "La primera obra que mando hacer fué una grande Cruz, que bendita, enarboló (ayudado de los Soldados y Sirvientes) y fixó en la mediania del tramo destinado para compás, que estaba enmediato a la Barraca de su habitacion, y otra que servia de interina Iglesia, siendo su compañia y todas sus delicias aquella sagrada Señal. Adorabala luego que amanecia, y cantaba la Tropa el Alabado, y delante de ella rezaba el Siervo de Dios Maytines y Prima, é inmediatamente celebraba el Santo Sacrificio de la Misa, a que asistian todos los Soldados y Mozos. Despues comenzaban todos su trabajo, cada uno en su destino, siendo Ingeniero y Sobrestante de la obra el V. Padre, quien muchas veces al dia adoraba la Santa Cruz, rezando delante de ella el oficio Divino."

[9]Palou, *Noticias,* II, 291-294. "Luego de concluida la fundacion de la mision de San Antonio de Padua pasó al real presidio de Monterey el reverendo padre presidente, y aunque deseaba con

and promote the work of the church and dwellings. With this purpose in view he journeyed to the banks of the Carmel, the first of August of the said year, 1771, accompanied by the five soldiers.

"The three sailors and four California Indians, assisted by the soldiers, had already cut timbers. Work was begun, and soon a small chapel was erected together with living quarters of four rooms, a large room for a granary, and also a house to be used as a dwelling and kitchen for the boys. All were of wood and had flat roofs and were enclosed in a good stockade. In the corner of the square there was a house, also with a flat roof, for the soldiers, and near, some corrals for the cattle and stock. As the workers were few, and progress could not be rapid because all the tools and utensils were in the old mission joining the Royal Presidio, work was not finished and the removal was not completed until the last of December of the said year of 71, in which year all was moved, the two ministers of the mission remaining to say mass at the Royal Presidio until establishment of the new mission was entirely completed.

"After its removal the mission of San Carlos was in a pleasant location, situated on a hill with a view over an extensive plain, which promises abundant crops. It extends along the Carmel River whose waters flow all the year, for although in dry seasons the water is not very plentiful, in rainy seasons no crossing can be found. The plain has many trees, willow, and other kinds, blackberry bushes, and quantities of Castillian roses. Near by on the left, at the foot of the hill, is a good lake with so much water, especially in rainy seasons, that its banks cannot hold all that it receives from the hills, and at such times the water runs off in a large ditch to the sea, which is at a distance of little more than two gun shots, in a little bay south of the Punta de Pinos; but in dry seasons the lake holds a quantity of good water, and has some springs. In rainy seasons, a dam formed in part by the hill extending across the lake makes it easy to retain enough water for all irrigating purposes on the plain.

"The mission is surrounded by small hills with good pastures for all kinds of cattle; it has an abundance of firewood as well as timber for building purposes, such as pine, white elms, and some redwoods; and at a distance of less than a league there are many cypresses on the point called by the same name, on account of the abundance of the trees; it has a beautiful sky, although after the rains the clouds are thick; the

vivas ansias pasar á fundar la otra de San Luis Obispo, pero no era dable por la falta de soldados para escoltas, y así dió mano á trasladar la mision como le encargaba su escelencia; para ello dispuso que en el real permaneciese su padre compañero fray Juan Crespi, y los ministros destinados para San Luis, y su reverencia determinó pasar á vivir al paraje que habia señalado en el Carmelo para idear la obra de la iglesia y vivienda, como tambien para acalorarlo.

"Con este fin se mudó á las orillas del Carmelo á principio de Agosto de dicho año de 1771, escoltado de los cinco soldados, y habiendo ya cortado alguna madera los tres marineros y cuatro indios Californios, á lo que tambien ayudaban los señores soldados, dió principio á la obra haciendo por de pronto una pieza para capilla y á su continuacion vivienda con cuatro piezas y una mayor para troje como tambien una casa para la vivienda de muchachos y su cocina, todo de madera con su terrado cercado todo de buena estacada. En la esquina del cuadro de elle una casa tambien con su terrado para guardia de los soldados, y á la vista unos corrales para las bestias y ganados. Como eran pocos los trabajadores y no apuraba mucho por tener en la mision vieja contigua al real presidio todas las cargas y trastes pertenecientes á la mision, no se dieron prisa; por cuya razon no se dió por concluida la obra y no se efectuó la total mutacion hasta últimos de Diciembre de dicho año de 71, en que quedaron del todo mudados, quedando en el real los dos ministros de la mision diciendo misa hasta tanto se verificase la fundacion de la mision.

"Quedó la mision de San Carlos con esta traslacion en un ameno sitio, fundada sobre una loma que tiene á la vista un dilatado llano muy á propósito para siembras, que es toda la vega del rio Carmelo cuya agua corre toda el año, aunque en tiempo de secas no es mucha el agua, siendo así que en tiempo de aguas no da vado toda su caja, muy poblada de arboleda, sauces y otros palos con mucha zarzamora é infinidad de rosales de Castilla que están tambien muy poblados los campos; á mano izquierda tiene una buena laguna al pié de la loma de esta mision, con bastante agua, principalmente en tiempo de lluvias que no alcanza á mantener en su caja toda la que recibe de las lomas circunvecinas, y en dicho tiempo corre por una grande zanja hasta la mar que dista poco mas de dos tiros de fusil, que es la ensenadita de la banda del Sur de la punta de Pinos: pero en tiempo de secas mantiene dicha laguna su porcion de agua buena que en sí tiene unos veneros, y en tiempo de aguas con una presa de unas cien varas que es el tramo de la loma y el ancho de dicha laguna, parece seriá fácil retener bastante aqua para regar lo que quisiese del llano que tiene á la vista.

"Está la mision ceracada de lomerias con buenos pastos para toda especie de ganados; tiene abundancia de leña como tambien de madera para fabricar, como de pinos, álamos blancos y algunos palos colorados; y á una legua poco menos de distancia hay muchos cipreses en la punta llamada de dichos árboles por la abundancia de ellos; tiene hermosa cielo, aunque despues de concluidas las aguas abundan las neblinas; la vista que tiene desde la mision á la mar es de dicha ensenada; en las cercanías de la mision hay varias rancherías de gentiles que desde luego de fundada la mision la empezaron á frecuentar y empezó en breve su reduccion, como diré en su lugar hablando del estado de dicha mision."

view looks out toward the sea upon the bay mentioned above; in the vicinity of the mission there are several rancherias of gentiles who, since the founding of the mission, have begun to frequent it. The mission within a short time began their conversion, as I shall tell in the account of the state of the mission."

Erection of Mission Buildings. In his first report, dated at the mission May 21, 1773, Fr. Serra gives the following description of the mission as it was at that time:[10]

"The first and most northerly, and consequently most remote, from this city, is the Mission of San Carlos de Monterey in the vicinity of the Rio Carmelo. This is the administrative head of the missions. It was founded Sunday, on the Feast of the Holy Ghost, 3d day of June, 1770, but as it was for an entire year incorporated with the Royal Presidio from which it was afterwards transferred to the place it now occupies, it is referred to as being established a year later.

"They first turned their attention to the building of the stockade and dwellings. This mission has a natural advantage over the others on account of its location among an abundance of the woods of various kinds, all easily obtained, and in its situation in a part where the soldiers so earnestly apply themselves to the work. To God praise be given!

"The stockade of rough timbers, thick and high with ravelins in the corners, is something more than seventy varas long and forty-three wide, and is closed at night with a key although it is not secure because of lack of nails. An entrance can easily be forced by the knocking off of timbers. The main house is seven varas wide and fifty long. It is divided into six rooms, all with doors and locks. The walls are made of rough timbers plastered over with mud both inside and out. Those of the principal rooms are whitewashed with lime. One of the rooms serves provisionally as a church.

"Near this building on the outside is the guard-house or barracks of the soldiers, and adjoining it, their kitchen. All are enclosed in the stockade. All of these buildings have flat roofs of clay and mud, and for most of them a kitchen has been made. There are various little houses for the Indians with straw or hay roofs. Attention was later given to a small garden which is near at hand, but for want of a gardener it has made little progress."

During the year 1774 a number of additional structures were built. According to the report of Father Serra, there had been erected during the year a house thirty by seven varas in size, constructed partly of adobe and partly of palisades with thatched roof. This was used as a workshop.

[10]Serra, Representacion de 21 de Mayo, 1773, in *Archivo de la Mision de Santa Barbara*, I, 92-93, *Archives of California, Provincial State Papers*, I, 109-111. "La primera y mas avanzada al Norte, y por tanto la mas remota de esta ciudad la de San Carlos de Monterey, en las cercanias del Rio Carmelo, Cabezera de las demas.

"Esta se fundio Domingo, y Pasoua del Espiritu Santo dia 3 de Junio de 1770, pero como estuvo un año entero incorporada al Real Presidio, de donde se transferió despues al lugar hoy tiene, se puede reputar como de un año menos de fundacion. A lo que primer se dió mano en el nuevo sitio, fué como se acostumbra á la Estacada y habitaciones. En uno y otro, ha quedado ventajosa a las demas como que la naturaleza aventajó el sitio en la abundancia de las maderas de varias especies, todas á la mano, y que es la parte en donde se aplicaron mas los soldados al trabajo. Dios se lo pague.

"La cerca ó Estacada de palos gruesos, tupidos, y altos con sus revellines en la Esquinas tiene de largo, algo mas de 70 varas, y de ancho 43 y se cierra de noche con la llave, ahunque por no estar enlatada por falta de clavos, es fácil con tumbor á desviar algun palo la entrada. La casa principal tiene de ancho 7 varas, y de largo 50 dividida en 6 piezas, todas con sus puertas y cerraduras. Las paredes de palos gruesos embarradas por fuera y por dentro, y las piezas principales blanqueadas con cal, una de las que sirve interinamente de iglesia.

"Junto a dha, cerca por la parte de afuera está la guardia ó cuartel de los soldados, y junto á él su cocina, ceñido uno y otro de su estacada. Todas dhas fabricas son de azotea de barro y tierra; y a mas de ellas se hizo nuestra cozina, y varias casitas para los Indios, con techos pajizos, o de zacate; se dio despues mano a una huertecita, que se cerco y por falta de hortelano hizo pocas medras."

Two other houses of about the same size as the one described were built, to be occupied by the families of two married servants. The surgeon and his family had another of similar size with a flat earth roof. It had two rooms together with a bedroom. Similar buildings housed the smith and his family, and the captain of the guard and his family, the latter building being of palisades with roof of straw. In addition to these buildings there had been erected a large oven of adobe for baking bread for the mission, and several smaller ones for the Indians.[11]

During the next twelve years there are but few recorded facts relating to the architectural history of the mission. It is inferred that activities continued without much change, the early structures still serving in large measure the purposes for which they had been erected.

Deaths of Fathers Crespi and Serra. During the years 1783 and 1784 the life of the mission was saddened by the deaths of its beloved founders, Father Crespi and Father Serra. Father Juan Crespi, who had been the faithful companion of Father Serra at Carmel since its first establishment, passed away early in 1783. He was a member of the party which founded San Diego in 1769, and served as chronicler of the Portolá expedition which discovered Monterey and San Francisco bays. He received his last sacrament at the hands of his old friend, companion, and superior, Father Junípero, and was buried within the sanctuary on the gospel side.[12]

The death of Fray Juan was severely felt by Father Serra, whose own health was rapidly failing. In spite of this, however, he again journeyed south by water in 1784, that he might begin his work of confirmation at San Diego, and pass northward through all the missions. His enfeebled condition showed that he was releasing his hold upon life and that his days of labor were nearly over. His deep concern in the success of the missions weighed heavily upon him. Realizing that his life was ebbing, representative priests from nearby missions were requested to gather about him, but Palou was the only one to reach San Carlos in time to be present at the death of the father president.

On the twenty-seventh of August, 1784, Serra stated that he would receive the Most Holy Viaticum in the church, although Palou advised the decoration of Serra's cell, assuring him that His Divine Majesty would come to visit him there. Father Serra replied in the negative, saying that he desired to receive it in the church, and since he was able to walk, there was no reason why his Lord should come to him. He went by himself to the

---

[11]Serra, Informe, 1774, in *Archivo de la Mision de Santa Barbara, Informes y correspondencia*, I, 146,147. (Bancroft Collection, ms.). "Desde el mes de Diciembre de 1773, que fué el primero y ultimo informe á V. Exc.ª del estado, y progressos de estas 5 misiones, hasta ultimos de Diciembre proximo pasado el 74 ha tenido esta mision los augmentos siguientes.

"Primeramente una casa de 30 varas de largo, y 7 de ancho parte de adobes, y parte de palizada, con su techo de zacate para oficina de, ____Otra dha de lo mismo, y del mismo tamaño para un sirviente casado. Otra dha algo mayor tambien de palizada con burrador con techo de zacate para otro sirviente casado con India de la Mision recien christiana. Otro dha de lo mismo con azotea de tierra, con dos piezas de sala y recamara para vivienda del cirujano y su familia. Otra dha de lo mismo y del mismo tamaño con sus 2 piezas para vivienda del herrero y su familia. Otra dha de palizada con techo de zacate en que vive el cabo de la escolta con su familia. Un horno de adobes para hacer pan. Unas hornillas de adoves para cozina de los Indios."

[12]Bancroft, *History of California*, I, 386.

church (a distance of more than one hundred varas) accompanied by the commander of the garrison. All the Indians of the village or mission accompanied the devoted sick father to the church with extreme tenderness and affection. Father Palou received from the lips of the dying padre the request that he be buried in the church, near Crespi.[13] He consequently was also buried within the sanctuary on the gospel side of the altar.[14] For a short time Palou succeeded to the presidency of the missions until the place was taken over by Father Lasuén of San Diego in November, 1785.[15]

San Carlos Visited by Lapérouse, 1786. In September, 1786, Monterey Bay was visited by Jean Francois Galaup de Lapérouse, then making a tour of the world for the purpose of obtaining geographical and other scientific information. For this purpose his expedition had been fitted out by the French government. The record left by Lapérouse gives a vivid and probably fairly accurate picture of the establishment as it was at that date He describes his visit to the mission as follows:[16]

"After traversing a small plain covered with herds of cattle, ... we ascended the hills, and were struck with the sound of several bells which announced our arrival, of which the monks had been apprized by a horseman whom the governor had detached for that purpose.

"We were received like lords of a parish when they make their first appearance on their estate; the president of the missions, clothed in his cope, the holy water sprinkler in his hand, waited for us at the door of the church, which was illuminated the same as on their greatest festivals; he conducted us to the foot of the high altar, where the *Te Deum* was sung in thanksgiving for the happy success of our voyage.

"Before we entered the church, we had passed by a place where the Indians of both sexes were ranged in a row; they expressed no surprise in their countenances, and we were left in doubt whether we were the subject of their conversation during the rest of the day. The parish church is very neat, although covered with straw; it is dedicated to Saint Charles, and ornamented with fairly good paintings, copied from Italian originals. There is a picture of Hell, in which the painter seems to have borrowed a little of the imagination of Callot; but as it is absolutely necessary to strike the senses of these new converts with the most lively impressions, I am persuaded that a similar representation has never done more service in any country, and that it would be impossible for the protestant mode of worship, which forbids images, and nearly all the other ceremonies of our church, to make any progress among this people. I have my doubts, whether the picture of Paradise, which is placed opposite to that of Hell, produces so good an effect on them; the state of quietness which it represents, and that complacent satisfaction of the elect who surround the throne of the Supreme Being, are ideas too sublime for rude unpolished man; but it is necessary to place rewards by the side of punishments, and it was a rigorous duty not to allow the smallest change in the kind of delights promised by the Catholic religion.

"We repassed, on going out of the church, the same row of male and female Indians, who had never quitted their post during the *Te Deum*; the children only had removed a little, and formed groups around the missionary's house, which is in

[13]Palou, *Vida*, 271-2, 274. "Deseo que me entierre en la iglesia cerquita del P. Fr. Juan Crespi por ahora, que quando se haga la iglesia de piedra me tiraran donde quisieren."

[14]Palou, *Vida*, 280. "Fué sepultado en el Presbyterio al lado del Evangelio."

[15]Payeras Report, 1818, in *Santa Barbara Archives*, XII, 453, Fages to Palou, 1785, in *Prov. Rec.*, III, 50, (Bancroft Collection, ms.).

[16]Lapérouse, *Voyage autour du monde* (Paris, 1798), II, 293-300.

front of the church, as are also the different storehouses. On the right stands the Indian village, consisting of about fifty cabins, which serve as dwelling places for seven hundred and forty persons of both sexes, including their children, which compose the mission of Saint Charles, or of Monterey.

"These cabins are the most miserable that are to be met with among any people; they are round, six feet in diameter, by four in height; some stakes, of the size of an arm, fixed in the earth, and which approach each other in an arch at the top, compose the timber-work of it; eight or ten bundles of straw, very ill arranged over these stakes, defend the inhabitants, well or ill, from the rain and wind; and more than half of this cabin remains open when the weather is fine; their only precaution is to have each of them two or three bundles of straw at hand by way of reserve.

"All the exhortations of the missionaries have never been able to procure a change of this general architecture of the two Californias; the Indians say that they like plenty of air, that it is convenient to set fire to their houses when they are devoured in them by too great quantity of fleas, and that they can build another in less than two hours. The independent Indians, who as hunters so frequently change their places of abode, have a stronger motive.

"The colour of these Indians, which is that of negroes; the house of the religious; their storehouses, which are built of brick and pointed with mortar; the floor of earth, upon which they press in the grain; the oxen, horses, in a word, everything reminded us of a habitation in Saint Domingo, or any other West India colony. The men and women are assembled by the sound of the bell, one of the religious conducts them to their work, to church, and to all their other exercises. . . . .

"The Indians as well as the missionaries rise with the sun, and go to prayers and mass, which last an hour, and during this time there is cooked in the middle of the square, in three large kettles, barley meal, the grain of which has been roasted previous to being ground; this species of boiled food, which the Indians call *atole*, and of which they are very fond, is seasoned neither with salt nor butter, and to us would prove a very insipid mess.

"Every cabin sends to take the portion for all its inhabitants in a vessel made of bark; there is not the least confusion or disorder, and when the coppers are empty, they distribute that which sticks to the bottom to the children who have best retained their lessons of catechism.

"This meal continues three quarters of an hour, after which they all return to their labours; some go to plough the earth with oxen, others to dig the garden; in a word, every one is employed in different domestic occupations, and always under the superintendence of one or two of the religious.

"The women are charged with little else but the care of their housewifery, their children, and roasting and grinding the several grains; this last operation is very long and laborious, because they have no other means of doing it but by crushing the grain in pieces with a cylinder upon a stone. M. de Langle, being a witness of this operation, made the missionaries a present of his mill, and a greater service could not have been rendered them, as by these means four women would in a day perform the work of a hundred, and time enough will remain to spin the wool of their sheep, and to manufacture coarse stuffs. But at present the religious, more occupied with the interests of heaven than temporal welfare, have greatly neglected the introduction of the common arts; they are themselves so austere, that they have no chimney to their chambers, though winter is frequently very severe there; and even the greater anchorites have never led a more edifying life."

Stone church erected, 1793–97. For more than twenty years temporary structures had served as a place of worship. Under the presidency of Lasuén a determined effort was made to replace the older by a permanent stone structure. During December, 1792, Manuel Estevan Ruíz, master mason and stone worker, took up his work at the Mission San Carlos. He was to instruct the natives in stonework and to supervise the construction of the buildings. As no material was then ready and as the heavy rainy season prevented the gathering of any sufficient amount, it was summer before the construction work upon the new church was actively started, the first stone being laid July 7, 1793.[17] Four years were consumed before the church building was completed. Finally in September, 1797, it was dedicated for service. It was described in the reports as being well built of cut stone (cantería), roofed with tile, and presenting a harmonious and beautiful appearance.[18]

Vancouver at San Carlos. During the time that the new church was under construction Captain George Vancouver of the British navy, while upon this coast, visited the mission in Carmel Valley. The artist of the expedition, J. Sykes, made a sketch of the establishment as it was at that time. This sketch (plate 2) is the first record to illustrate in pictorial form the appearance of the mission. Vancouver records his observations as follows:[19]

". . . . on Sunday the 2nd of December, in consequence of a very polite invitation, I paid my respects to the mission of St. Carlos, accompanied by Senr. Quadra. Senr. Arguella, Senr. Caamano, Mr. Broughton, and several other English and Spanish officers.

"This establishment is situated about a league to the south-eastward of the presidio of Monterey. The road between them lies over some steep hills and hollow vallies, interspersed with many trees; the surface was covered over with an agreeable verdure; the general character of the country was lively, and our journey altogether was very pleasant. . . . .

"The usual ceremonies on introduction being over, our time was pleasantly engaged in the society of the father president and his two companions, the priests regularly belonging to the mission of St. Carlos, who attended us over their premises. These seemed to differ but little from those at St. Francisco, or Sta. Clara; excepting that the buildings were smaller, the plan, architecture, and materials exactly corresponding.

[17]Lasuén to Borica, San Carlos, Dec. 10, 1794, in *Archivo de la Mision de Santa Barbara,* VI, 219-220; Lasuén to Arrillaga, June 7, 1794, in *Archivo del Arzobispado,* I, 38. (Bancroft Collection, ms.). It is probable that Serra and Crespi had much to do with the designing of the later stone church. Father Serra made definite reference to the stone church in arranging for his burial (*note* 13). It should be borne in mind that the experiences of both of these men in Sierra Gorda had prepared them for church building as well as religious work. In the valley of Tilaco Crespi had constructed the Mission of San Francisco including a large church of stone "with its vaulted ceiling (bovedas) and tower" (Palou, *Vida,* 237; James edition, 230). Serra had spent seven years in constructing a large church at the Mission of Jalpan. It was more than one hundred forty-seven feet long and thirty feet wide and was built of rubble work. It is described as having a transcept and dome and a suitable sacristy with vaulted ceiling. (*Vida,* 34; James edition, 32).

[18]*Archives of California, State Papers Missions,* II, 5; Lasuén Estado General, 1793-4, San Carlos, Mar. 11, 1795, in *Archivo de la Mision de Santa Barbara,* XII, 57. "La iglesia de la Mision de S. Carlos se concluyó en el presente año; es toda de cantería; su techo es de teja y está bien provista de ornamentos y útiles. . . ." Sal, *Estado,* Monterey, Dec. 31, 1797, in *Archives of California, State Papers Missions,* II, 120. "La iglesia de San Carlos se bendijo y dedico por Sept de 97 y esta buena." *Lasuén Report,* 1797-8, San Carlos, Feb. 20, 1799, in *Archivo de la Mision de Santa Barbara,* XII, 66. (Bancroft Collection, ms.).

[19]Vancouver, *A Voyage of Discovery,* II, 33-36. There appears to be a serious discrepancy between Vancouver and Lasuén in reference to the date when the construction of the mission church was begun. Vancouver gives the date of his visit as Dec. 2, 1792, and proceeds to describe the materials and methods used in building the church which he found in process of construction. On the other hand, Lasuén says the head mason did not arrive at Carmel until after that date and that six months more elapsed before the first stone was laid. It is probable, therefore, that Vancouver may have confused the dates of his visit. He was at Monterey again in November and December, 1794, and it is possible his notes and sketch may belong to that date rather than to the earlier visit, *ibid.,* III, 324-340. This is the opinion of Bancroft.

PLATE 1. *Forest of Monterey Pines.* Moran, photo.

The value of this forest was noted by Vizcaíno and Crespi. From it Serra obtained the timbers for San Carlos Mission.

PLATE 2. *San Carlos Mission, 1794.* Sketch by Sykes.

This is the earliest pictorial representation of the mission. Since it is a sketch it must not be considered as having the same degree of accuracy in detail as a photograph. It will be seen that the church was being constructed, as mentioned by Vancouver, and that there were numerous buildings around an open plaza. Three crosses are shown, one in the plaza to the right, a larger one in the court at the left, and another surmounting a building at the extreme left. The larger cross may have been the one erected by Serra in 1771.

"In their granaries were deposited a pretty large quantity of the different kinds of grain before noticed at the other establishments, to which was added some barley, but the whole was of an inferior quality, and the return from the soil by no means equal to that produced at Sta. Clara. Here also was a small garden on the same confined scale, and cultivated in the same manner as observed at the other stations.

"An Indian village is also in the neighborhood; it appeared to us but small, yet the number of its inhabitants under the immediate direction of this mission was said to amount to eight hundred, governed by the same charitable principles as those we had before visited. Notwithstanding these people are taught and employed from time to time in many of the occupations most useful to civil society, they had not made themselves any more comfortable habitations than those of their forefathers; nor did they seem in any respect to have benefited by the instruction they had received. Some of them were at this time engaged under the direction of the fathers, in building a church with stone and mortar. The former material appeared to be of a very tender friable nature, scarcely more hard than indurated clay; but I was told, that on its being exposed to the air, it soon becomes hardened, and is an excellent stone for the purpose of building. It is of a light straw colour, and presents a rich and elegant appearance, in proportion to the labour that is bestowed upon it. It is found in abundance at no great depth from the surface of the earth; the quarries are easily worked, and it is I believe the only stone the Spaniards have hitherto made use of in building. At Sta. Clara I was shown a ponderous black stone, that father Thomas said was intended to be so appropriated as soon as persons capable of working it could be procured. The lime they use is made from sea shells, principally from the ear shell, which is of a large size and in great numbers on the shores; not having as yet found any calcareous earth that would answer this essential purpose. The heavy black stone is supposed to be applicable to grinding, and should it be found so to answer, it will be a matter of great importance to their comfort, since their only method of reducing their corn to flour is by two small stones placed in an inclined position on the ground; on the lower one the corn is laid, and ground by hand by rubbing the other stone nearly of the same surface over it. The flour produced by this rude and laborious process makes very white and well tasted, though heavy bread, but this defect is said by the Spaniards to be greatly remedied when mixed with an equal proportion of flour properly ground.

"After we had satisfied our curiosity in these particulars we rode round the neighborhood of the mission. It was pleasantly situated, and the country, agreeably broken by hills and vallies, had a verdant appearance, and was adorned like that in the vicinity of Monterrey, with many clumps and single trees, mostly of the pine tribe, holly-leaved oak and willows; with a few trees of the poplar and maple, and some variety of shrubs, that rather incommoded our travelling, which was chiefly confined to one of the vallies, and within sight of the buildings. Through this valley a small brook of water about knee-deep, called by the Spaniards Rio Carmelo, takes its course, passes the buildings of the mission, and immediately empties itself into the sea.

"In this valley, near the sides of the Carmelo, a few acres of land exhibited a tolerably good plant of wheat; but as the soil here, as well as at Monterrey, is of a light sandy nature, its productions are consequently inferior to the other two missions I had visited; yet I was given to understand, that the interior country here, like that at St. Francisco, improves in point of fertility, as it retires from the ocean.

"On our return to the convent, we found a most excellent repast served with great neatness, in a pleasant bower constructed for that purpose in the garden of the mission."

Elsewhere it is stated that in December, 1793, while in San Diego, Vancouver presented the president of the mission with a "handsome barrelled organ" for the use and ornament of the new church which was being built at the presidency of the missions at San Carlos.[20]

The Quarters of the Neophytes, 1800. In his report for 1800 Father Lasuén, the president of the missions, describes the nature of the dwellings used by the Christianized Indians, criticism of which has been seen in the descriptions by both Lapérouse and Vancouver. He also describes in some detail the dormitory of the girls and unmarried women. The report reads as follows:[21]

"Although the houses of the Neophytes do not differ in material and form from those which the Gentiles use, they are indeed different in cleanliness and good condition. Ordinarily the missionaries and also the Christian Indians continue improving the arrangement of their houses and rarely will one condescend to live in a small hut like he had in his Gentilism. In the channel of Santa Barbara the natives never use similar small huts. They have always, in contrast with the remainder of those in subjection, houses sufficiently roomy. They are built of paling and thatch and because of this exposed to fire. It is well known that for many years neither in missions, nor in pueblos, nor in presidios had there been churches, dwellings nor storerooms of any other material. Of the latter some rooms are still preserved, in many places as in the royal presidio of San Francisco almost all. Accordingly, as they have been able, or as they now find themselves able they construct buildings of adobe or of stone roofed with tile. In this manner are the houses of the Indians (I do not know how this has been reported by the Governor or any of the commandants) of San Francisco and Santa Clara built. Many are furnished with metates, earthen pans, round pots, stewing pans and even little ovens for cooking bread, while others have much more than these.

"The girls and the unmarried women (wrongly called nuns) are gathered together and locked up at night in their quarters. This provision is taken for convenience and it may be said for necessity, for all possible care is taken that nothing may compromise their safety. It has been observed that rarely do those in this rank and station die, nor do they run away and take refuge in the mountains. They have spacious rooms furnished with chairs and with sufficient ventilation. Here in San Carlos (and the same will happen in other missions) they have changed their dormitory many times, seeking each time better accomodation until they have been able to construct the form desired by the missionaries.

---

[20]Vancouver, *A Voyage of Discovery,* II 472. This organ was still in use in 1837, when Du Petit-Thouars visited the mission.

[21]Representation, Nov. 12, 1800, in *Archivo de la Mision de Santa Barbara,* II, 179-181. "Aunque los Alojmtos de los Neofitos no se diferencian en sus materiales, y en su formacion de los que usan los Gentiles, pero si en la limpieza, y buena condicion, de el regularmte andan los Missioneros y aun tambien los Christianos mejorando la disposicion de sus casas, y raro sera el que se acomode ya a vivir en choza estrecha, como la que tenia en su Gentilidad. En el Canal de Sta Barbara nunca usaron los naturales semejtes chozas estrechas, spre tubieron a diferencia de los restantes de esta conquista viviendo suficientemte capaces. Si son ahora como antes de palisada, y zacate, y pr eso expuestas al incendio, es bien sabido que en muchos años, ni en misiones ni en pueblos, ni en presidios tuvo iglesias abitaciones, ni oficianas de otra calidad. Y de esta misma se conserva todabia algunas piezas, en muchas partes que y en el Rl presidio de Sn Franco casi todas. Segun se ha podido, y se va pudiendo se hacen fabricas de adove, o de piedra techadas de teja. Asi estan ya, [no se como no lo ha dho el Sor. Govor. o algo de los Comandtes] las casas de los Indios, de Sn. Franco, y Sta. Clara, surtidas muchas de mas, y se iran surtiendo las otras de metates, comales, ollas cazuelas ye hta de ornitos pa cocer pan. . . . A lo mismo se aspira en las demas misiones.

"Las muchachas y solteras [Monjas pr mal nombre] se recogen, y se encierran de noche en un cuarto. Si esta providencia se toma pr convte y puede decirse pr necesaria, se cuida todo lo que es posibe que no sea en perjuicio de su salud. Efectivamte, se ha observado, que rara de las de este estado, y regimen se mueren, si no es de las que dan en huirse, y retirarse al monte. Se tienen pa eso piezas capaces, asendas, y de correspondte ventilacion. Aqui en Sn. Carlos, [y sucedera lo mismo en otras missiones] se les mudo muches veces el dormitorio, buscando cada vez mejor comodidad hta que llego el tpo de poderlo hacer segun el deceo de los misioneros.

"Es por cierto en el dia la mejor pieza, que fuera de la Iglesia tiene la mission de 17 varas de largo en claro, mas de seis de ancho, y otro tanto de alto: paredes de adobe y medio, enjarradas de mezcla y blanqueadas; un entarimado fuerte, y bien labrado, corrido pr los dos costados y pr una testera, de mas de vara de alto, y mas de dos de ancho, tres ventanas grandes con sus rejas torneadas, pr un lado, y quatro troneras pr otro, su lugar comun es pr separado, y todo con buena vigueria cubierta con tablazon, y techo de teja."

PLATE 3. *San Carlos Mission, 1823.* Sketch by Wm. Smythe.

This sketch appears in various forms. This has been taken from an engaving published by Forbes in his *History of California* in 1839. It gives a much more comprehensive idea of the mission than does the Sykes sketch and if not followed with too slavish attention to detail may be taken as very satisfactory. Several buildings are to be seen upon the hill to the right of the mission church, while to the left is shown a portion of the building enclosing the quadrangle. The road from Monterey is shown in the foreground together with a cross which may have marked the way to the mission.

PLATE 4. *San Carlos Mission, 1839.* From Laplace.

Fortunately the artist in this case chose a point of observation not usually taken and has therefore preserved for us a view of the mission from the hill to the rear of the mission grounds. It shows the enclosed court and indicates that the buildings around the court were more than one story in height. Since it is merely a sketch, care must be taken not to place too much emphasis upon details, especially if these are in conflict with other evidence.

29

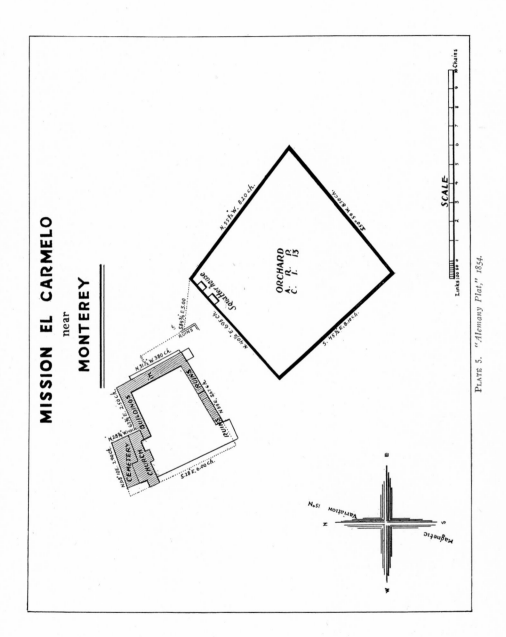

MISSION EL CARMELO
near
MONTEREY

ORCHARD
A. R. P.
C. I. 13

Squatter house

RUINS

CHURCH

CEMETERY

WITH BUILDINGS

RUINS

SCALE

Links 100 50 0   Chains

Magnetic

Variation 15°

PLATE 5. "*Alemany Plat,*" 1854.

30

"It is a fact that the best room which the mission has, besides the church, is 17 varas long in the clear, more than 6 wide and as much more in height; walls an adobe and a half in thickness plastered over with mortar and whitewashed; a strong and well-made boarded floor, extended on two sides and on the front, of more than a vara in height and more than two in width, three large windows with round iron gratings, on one side, and four smaller windows on the other, . . . the whole covered with heavy cross beams and planks with a roof of tiles."

The Mission Quadrangle. The report for the year 1815 records that several buildings had been constructed, thus enclosing the quadrangle or court of the mission.[22] In 1818 a small chapel was built adjoining the church. According to the report of Fr. Payeras it was known as "la capilla a la Pasion del Señor," and was built not only as a place of devotion but also to preserve the older building from the fury of the strong south winds. It was provided with an altar and painted wood carvings.[23]

Erection of the "Via Crucis," 1820. For the year 1820 the report mentions several improvements at the mission. Two bells had been provided and several buildings painted. The approach to the church had been adorned with a "Via Crucis."[24] This latter is more fully described by later observers. Capt. F. W. Beechey, who visited Monterey in December, 1827, thus describes the approach to the mission:[25]

"The ride from the presidio to San Carlos on a fine day is most agreeable. The scenery is just sufficiently picturesque to interest, while the hills are not so abrupt as to inconvenience a bold rider. The road leads principally through fine pasture lands, occasionally wooded with tall pine, oak, and birch trees; but without any underwood to give it a wildness, or to rob it of its park-like aspect. Before the valley of San Carmelo opens out, the traveller is apprized of his approach to the mission by three large crosses erected upon Mount Calvary; and further on by smaller ones placed at the side of the road, to each of which some history is attached."

Alvarado says a portion of the road from Monterey to San Carlos was known as that of Calvary, that twelve crosses were planted along the road at equal distances representing the twelve stations of the "Via Crucis," and that on Good Friday appropriate religious services were always celebrated.[26]

Secularization of the Mission. The best days of San Carlos were over. The annual reports make mention of the buildings only to speak of their sad condition. In 1824 the houses and workshops had their roofs renewed,

[22]"Se han hecho 50 varas de fabrica, las que faltaban para cerrar el quadro, y plaza de la mision y se han remendado las fabricas anteriores." Informe de San Carlos, Dec. 31, 1815, in *Archivo de las Misiones,* I, 372.

[23]Informe de San Carlos, Dec. 31, 1818, in *Archivo Misiones, Papeles Originales,* I, 432; and Payeras report of May 4, 1819, "La [mision], de San Carlos ha eregido contigua a la iglesia una capilla a la Pasion del Señor que exista a devocion y preserva de los fuertos sures a la fabrica vieja," in *Archivo de Santa Barbara,* XII, 98. (Bancroft Collection, ms.)

[24]Informe de San Carlos, Dec. 31, 1820, in *Archivo de las Misiones, Papeles Originales,* I, 328 (Bancroft Collection, ms.). "Se han puesto dos campañas la una grande de 36 @, [probably arroba, equivalent to 25 pounds], y la otra mediana de 27 @; se ha adornado a iglesia con una Via Crucis y se han pintado tres colaterales.

[25]Beechey, *Narrative of a Voyage to the Pacific,* 343.

[26]Hittell. *History of California,* I, 639-640. One of these crosses may be seen in the Smythe sketch of 1823. (Plate 3.)

but the walls of the garden were down and other repairs were needed.[27] This decline in the prosperity of the mission was due not only to conditions within the missions themselves but also and in larger measure to the manner in which they were treated by the Mexican government. In January, 1831, a decree of secularization was issued by Echeandía. According to this order San Carlos and San Gabriel were to be organized at once into towns, the surplus property after distribution to the neophytes passing under the control of secular administrators.[28]

A change in administration whereby Echeandía was displaced by Manuel Victoria prevented the putting of this order into effect,[29] and the controversy regarding the secularization of the California missions continued for some years longer. Finally on November 4, 1834, the act of secularization was adopted and announced by Governor Figueroa. By it San Carlos and Monterey were combined as a curacy of the first class.[30] In accordance with the plan of secularization an inventory was made of the property of the various missions. That of San Carlos, dated December 10, 1834, valued the mission property at approximately $46,022. Of this the church itself is estimated at $10,000; the furniture, vestments, library, etc., at $10,217.[31]

San Carlos in Ruins, 1836–41. In October, 1836, the United States ship "Peacock" stopped at Monterey on its way from the Orient where Mr. Edmund Roberts as special agent of the United States government had been engaged in a diplomatic mission. A visit was made to the San Carlos mission which is described as follows:[32]

"At this time there are twenty-one missions in Upper California, all of which are in a state of decay. I visited that at Carmelo, which I found in ruins, and almost abandoned. It is about four miles from Monte-rey. The road to it is easy, and agreeably varied by hill and dale, everywhere covered by pine and other forest trees, and remarkably free from undergrowth.

"The mission building is, perhaps, a hundred yards square, one story high, and roofed with tiles. We rode through the gate, which was just ready to fall from its hinges, into the great central court, round which it is built, where we found eight or ten Indians engaged in repairing the roof. They informed us that the Padre was at the presidio, or garrison, and that there was no one to show us the church, which, exteriorly, was in a dilapidated state. All the windows opened in upon the court, and were heavily barred with iron, with the design of preventing the escape of the christian neophytes, who were locked up at night in apartments to which these windows give light and air. Some of those were open. They were strewed with rubbish and filth, and, altogether, in a worse condition than the commonest stable should be."

[27]Informe de San Carlos, Dec. 31, 1822, in *Archivo de las Misiones, Papeles Originales,* I, 555, 1824, *Ibid,* I, 759 (Bancroft Collection, ms.). "En la iglesia y sacristia existen los [utensilios], de los años anteriores, a excepcion de algunas cosas de poca consideracion que se ha disparecido y se procura de poner y se ha anadido un crucifijo grande cuatro santos de talla grande que son N. S. P. S. Franco, St. Domingo, S. Buenaventura y St. Clara. La casa y demas oficinas se han techado, no se ha hecho fabrica ninguna. Las parades en la huerta se han caido, veremos si se pueden levantar del año. Las herramientas en casa y campo poco mas o menos subsisten como los años anteriores."

[28]Bancroft, III, 305-6.

[29]*Ibid,* III, Chaps. XI, XII; **Richman,** *California Under Spain and Mexico,* 228 et seq.; Engelhardt, III, 311-360.

[30]Engelhardt, III, 531.

[31]*Ibid,* III, 534.

[32]Ruschenberger, *A Voyage round the world, in 1835, 1836 and 1837* (Philadelphia, 1838), 507.

The next year the French explorer Abel Du Petit-Thouars was along this coast and visited the ruins of the mission in Carmel Valley. His description of the condition of the establishment as seen at that time is as follows:[33]

"Upon our arrival at the mission of San Carlos we were struck by the solitude of the place and by the state of ruin in which the buildings were found. The grounds surrounding this establishment, formerly covered with rich crops, did not offer more to the eye than a picture of the most complete sterility. Through a little door we entered a large court shaped like a parallelogram; this court is enclosed on three sides by the dwellings of the neophytes; the fourth is occupied by the storerooms for the reserve food supply. A large wooden cross still stood in the center of this enclosure. In one of the corners of the court is the church, the principal door of which opens on the field outside of the mission, but one is able to communicate with the establishment by means of a small lateral chapel. We saw no one upon entering the court of the mission: it was deserted! the lodgings were without doors and windows and the roofs, broken in many places, were already giving way under their own weight. On visiting the part at the north of the mission we entered a large room, dark and without furniture, where we met Father *Jose-Maria del Real,* the sole surviving ecclesiastic at the mission: that religious was one of those who had been sent out from the college of Zacatecas. After a reception at first dubious, he recovered from the surprise which our appearance had caused him; he became very polite and with great courtesy showed us about the ruins: we visited with him the ruined buildings in the midst of which he lived without society, and, judging from appearances, very miserably. Two or three families of Indians, fixed by habit, still lived in the ruins which surrounded the mission. . . . The garden of the mission, situated on the ground which stretches out in a gentle slope from the mission to the edge of the river Carmelo, offers scarcely any signs of cultivation. Formerly very fertile, the garden produced in abundance all the vegetables and fruits necessary not only for the establishment, but also for the town of Monterey and for vessels in port. At present it is entirely abandoned, the fence no longer remains, and the few fruit trees which are still to be seen here yield scarcely any produce, and that is always consumed before it attains a suitable degree of maturity.

"Afterwards we went to visit the church, entering through the lateral chapel which gives access to the church through the court of the mission. Upon entering the chapel I noticed several paintings on wood which represented subjects delineated in the holy scriptures; but my attention was particularly attracted by the sight of a large painting of *San Isidro el labrador* [patron of the laborers], which is at the left upon entering the chapel. It was hanging at an angle by one of the upper corners of the frame. In this position the saint and his plough looked upside down. Our reverend guide, after having pointed out to me the painting to the right, made three genuflections and as many signs of the cross and afterwards appeared absorbed in profound meditation from which I could scarcely rouse him. I wished to know the reason for these particular devotions, suspecting that a little of the supernatural might well have become mingled with an event in itself perfectly natural. At last, pressed by me to declare this mystery, the reverend father, in a tone of great sorrow and in a deep voice, informed me that during an earthquake this picture had been thus disarranged and that surely this catastrophe had been the manifestation of the will of God and a definite prediction of the ruin of the missions. After these words the brother, don Jose, crossed himself again and relapsed into his pious reveries! Until recently there could be seen in the church a picture which represented La Perouse arriving at the mission of San Carlos

---

[33]Du Petit-Thouars, *Voyage autour du monde sur la fregate La Venus, pendant les annees 1836-1839.* II, 116-120. Translated from the French text.

and the brilliant reception which was tendered him by all the mission: this picture disappeared at the time of the departure of the Spanish missionaries. . . .

"We also saw in the church a portable organ given at one time by Captain Vancouver to the president of the missions of California whom he met at the port of San Diego. That organ, of an extreme Gothic type, must have been very beautiful: it was not yet entirely out of service."

The next recorded visit to the mission was made by Laplace, a French traveler in 1839. The author does not discuss the mission but fortunately incorporates a sketch of the establishment as it was seen at that time.[34] This sketch is herewith reproduced (plate 4).

When visited in 1841 by Duflot de Mofras, the ruin of the mission was complete, the padre even having removed to the neighboring town of Monterey. He speaks of the mission as follows:[35]

"The mission of Mount Carmel, situated at the northern extremity of the Sierra de Santa Lucia and hemmed in by the mountains, is no longer a flourishing institution. In 1834 it still assembled five hundred neophytes; it had three thousand horned cattle, seven hundred horses, seven thousand sheep and harvested fifteen hundred fanegas of grain. Today all has gone; under the pretext of forming a pueblo in the vicinity, the mission was allowed to fall in ruins. The Indian population is composed of not more than thirty individuals. This establishment, as also the one at Soledad, lying nearest the seat of government, was one of the first to be despoiled. The missionary in charge of Carmel now resides at Monterey."

Under American Control. In July, 1846, the American flag was raised at Monterey by the forces of the United States Navy. This change in jurisdiction was fully recognized by the treaty of 1848 whereby the territory was definitely ceded by Mexico.

Already a number of American settlers had immigrated to California, but the discovery of gold in 1848 caused an unprecedented rush to the new region. Among these people were many who recorded their observations in articles or books and thus give descriptions of the incidents, scenes and places of interest that attracted their attention. Many of them give accounts of the missions. Unfortunately most of these writings are a mixture of vague historical accounts with indefinite descriptions of the ruined missions, one pleasing exception to this being the account given by J. R. Bartlett of the United States and Mexican Boundary Commission, who visited Monterey in April, 1852. He says:[36]

"The Mission establishment, which consists of a church and the usual accompaniments of a large inclosure with ranges of small buildings, stands upon a little elevation between the hills and the sea, from which it is distant only a few hundred yards. The church which is built of stone, has two towers, containing six bells; its walls are very thick, with an arched roof, and supported by heavy buttresses. The towers, as usual, differ. The adobe buildings near, were all in a state of ruin, and tenantless; not a human being was to be seen near, while the rank grass and weeds which monopo-

[34]Laplace, *Campagne de circumnavigation de la fregate l'Artemise, pendant les annees 1837, 1838, 1839 and 1840.* (Paris, 1841-54), vi, 294.

[35]Duflot de Mofras, *Exploration du territoire de l'Oregon, des Californies et de la mer Vermeille, executee pendant les annees 1840, 1841 et 1842.* (Paris, A. Bertrand, 1844). I. 391-2. Translated from the French.

[36]Bartlett, *Personal Narrative*, II, 77.

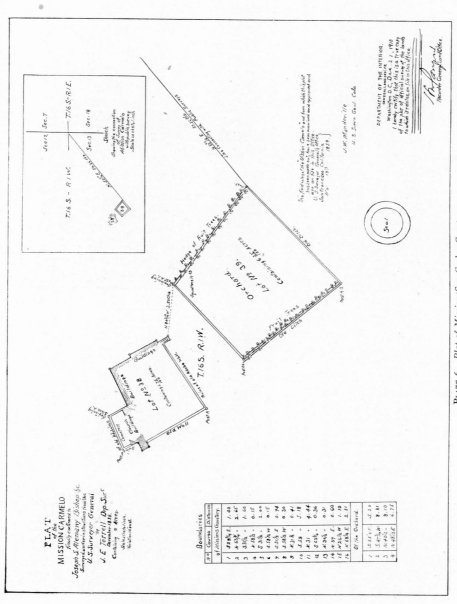

PLATE 6. Plat of Mission San Carlos Grant.

35

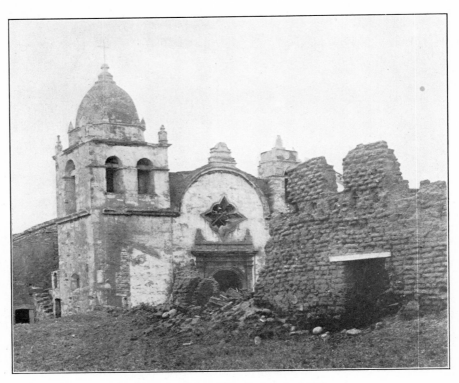

PLATE 7. *Ruins of San Carlos, about 1876.*

This photograph by Muybridge is a very early picture of the mission ruins and is of value in that it gives many items of detail regarding the buildings in front of and adjoining the church. The ruined wall in the foreground to the right retained the doorway leading into the court, while it also shows the floor timbers and windows for the rooms of the second floor. The markings upon the front of the church show plainly the height and slant of the roof line.

PLATE 8. *Restoration of San Carlos Mission by Oriana Day, 1884.*

This must not be taken as of the same value as the photographs, or sketches, but merely as an attempt of an artist to reproduce a scene at the mission as it had been described. It is said to represent the ideas of General M. G. Vallejo as he saw the mission before the time of secularization.

lized the ground, showed that even curiosity did not often tempt visitors to its deserted precincts. One corner of the church began to show the ravages of time: its cornice had fallen, and weeds had already taken root among its opening crevices. The remains of an orchard and vineyard, are still seen near, in a decaying state. Small pine trees cover the hills within a short distance of the church; and on its other side, the ocean rolls up its waves with a dull monotonous sound, which adds to the solitary feeling of the place."

Title Confirmed to Church, 1859. Whereas it had been the plan of the Mexican government, under the excuse of secularization, to exploit the missions and place their property for sale, it became the policy of the United States government to confirm to the church authorities full title to those lands that had been used for religious purposes, such as the church site, burial grounds, orchards and gardens. In accordance with this policy the United States Land Commission awarded to Bishop J. S. Alemany, as head of the Catholic Church in California, the title to a tract of land containing nine acres known as Mission Carmelo. The land was first surveyed by the church authorities in 1854 when presenting their claims before the United States District Court (plate 5). This is the first survey extant of the mission buildings and lands. An official survey (plate 6) was made by the United States government in December, 1858, and formed the basis for the issuance of the patent which was granted the church authorities October 19, 1859.[37]

Later Descriptions and Photographs. The ruins of San Carlos, the roof of which fell in during the year 1852,[38] continued to attract people interested in the romantic and picturesque. Mr. H. H. Bancroft, after a visit to the mission in 1874, wrote the following description of the church as it then appeared:[39]

"The church is strong and well built, of irregularly hewn stone with a timbered roof on which had been laid brush or stick and covered with tiles. The building was in a state of ruins, part of the roof was off but most of the walls were standing. It is

[37]The "Alemany Plat," so called, is preserved with the plats of the other twenty missions in the Archives of the United States District Court, San Francisco. Plate 5 is a reproduction of this document. Since all the other plats accompanying this one indicate the survey as having been made during the fall of 1854, that date is assumed for this also. It is to be noted that this plat gives more definite information regarding the quadrangle buildings than does the United States Survey made four years later.

The second plat is herewith reproduced (plate 6) as preserved in the Surveyor General's Archives, San Francisco. The field notes describing the mission buildings are taken from the Monterey County Archives and read as follows: "Beginning at a stake marked 'A. 1.' at the northeast corner of the cemetery. Thence . . . south 28° 45' east, 95 links [62.7 feet] to the corner of the Church Buildings, 1.40 chains [92.1 feet] to station, at the angle formed by the church and adjoining buildings. Thence, along the line of buildings 63° east 2.65 chains [175 feet] to station at a corner of the buildings. Thence south 31° 30' east, 1.60 chains [105.6 feet] to station, at corner as above. Thence north 58° 30' east, 15 links [9.92 feet] to station at corner as above. Thence south 31° 30' east, 2 chains [132 feet] to station at corner as above. Thence south 58° 30' west, 15 links [9.92 feet] to station at corner as above. Thence south 31° 30' east, 74 links [48.8 feet] to station at corner above. Thence south 58° 30' west, 30 links [19.8 feet] to station at corner as above Thence north 31° 30' west, 41 links [27.1 feet] to station at Old Adobe Wall. Thence along the ruins of an old adobe wall south, 59° west, 5.18 chains [342 feet] to a point marked 'A' station. Thence north 31° west, 4.44 chains [293 feet] to station at point of intersection of the old wall with a row of church buildings. Thence along the line of church buildings south 63° 45' west, 36 links [23.6 feet] to station at corner of buildings. Thence north 30° 30' west 51 links [33.66 feet] to station at corner of buildings. Thence north 57° east, 60 links [39.6 feet] to station at corner of buildings. Thence north 26° 15' west, at 40 links [26.4 feet] leaves the line of church buildings and along the ruins of the old adobe wall of the cemetery, 1.10 chains [72.5 feet] to a point marked 'A' station. Thence along the north boundary of the cemetery, north 68° 15' east, 2.51 chains [165.66 feet] to the point of beginning." *Archives of the Recorder, Patents A,* 435-436.

[38]Hutchings, *California Magazine,* IV (1859-60), 496.

[39]H. H. Bancroft. *Personal observations,* 1874, p. 210-211.

10 by 56 varas, the sacristy 7 by 14 varas. The walls were built without lime with an adobe mortar, except the finer ornamented stone work about the doors and windows which were put together with cement, or lime mortar. Six stone arches two feet wide thrown over head forming part of the ceiling still remained standing, though apparently ready to fall without much warning, threads of tottering stone-work. Bent pieces of timber overlaid the stone arches."

Fortunately new elements now appear which have been found of great value to those now interested in reconstructing the missions. In the place of vague descriptions and sketches whose accuracy is open to serious question, lovers of bygone days began to take a more scientific interest in preserving a true record of the state of the missions as they had been in their prime, the camera also began to come into use with exact photographic reproductions of such ruins as remained. In this manner many important details overlooked by the writers and now long since obliterated have been preserved for all time.

Among the earlier artists and photographers who have shown a special interest in the missions several names should be mentioned. Among these are Eduard Vischer, C. W. J. Johnson, C. E. Watkins, E. J. Muybridge, Perkins, Fiske and Taber, all of whom have made valuable contributions.[40] First in time, if not in importance, is Eduard Vischer, whose mission sketches constitute a most valuable legacy. Three of these sketches are views of San Carlos; unfortunately, however, since they are among his earliest work they do not give as much information as one would desire. Writing in 1872, he says of San Carlos:[41]

"This mission, after an occupation of half a century, was, like others subsequent to the secularization neglected, and finally abandoned—and now only exhibits deserted walls. Besides the natural causes of dilapidation, vandalism was at work, wantonly defacing the interior of the church; more than all, the antiquarian mania and destructive energy of one of the Monterey priests, who, in the fruitless search for Father Junipero's remains, upturning the graves of several generations, removed the altar, and, as a precaution against accident to the workmen there employed, had a great portion of the roof taken off, which was never replaced, and, subsequently, the rafters, tiles, and all serviceable material were carried off for the use of neighboring settlers."

The reference to vandalism is amplified in a note which states that "on the occasion of modern clam and chowder picnics and whisky sprees, more than once bonfires were lighted in the deserted church, using door frames and paneling as convenient fuel." At other times mounted men rode through the buildings amusing themselves firing their revolvers at the images and other objects.

---

[40]Some of Johnson's photographs are reproduced in the frontispiece and by plates 11 and 12. Plate 7 is from a Muybridge photograph, plates 10 and 41 from Fiske, plate 9 from Watkins and plate 21 from Perkins.

[41]Vischer, *Missions of Upper California,* 1872, (San Francisco, 1872), appendix i-ii. He first visited California in 1842. At that time, while many of the missions had been practically abandoned, they still gave evidence of the greatness of earlier days. He again came to California with the gold seekers and in 1861 began the task of preserving by means of carefully executed sketches the record of the missions as they then were. Archives were consulted and ruin heaps carefully examined in order that the work might be done with accuracy. The collection was completed in 1878.

PLATE 9. *San Carlos Church before 1880.*

This enlargement from a stereo by Watkins is valuable not only as showing the condition of the church at the date indicated but also for other features of detail. The most striking feature is probably the exposed arch supporting the roof. Attention is also called to the remains of a wall in the foreground to the left and to the doorway into the dome on the larger tower. This is reproduced from a stereograph in the State Library.

PLATE 10. *San Carlos Church about 1882.*

This is a view similar to the preceding, but taken at a later date, is evidenced by the more ruined condition of the roof. Attention is here called to the cross timbers, the ends of which are visible along the stone walls; to the buttresses, which are also well reproduced; as well as the remains of the high wall around the smaller burial ground. It should also be noted in this as in the preceding photograph that the sacristy had been covered by a roof of shakes at an earlier date. This is a Fiske photograph (No. 601) from a copy made by Mr. C. B. Turrill from his collection.

PLATE 11.   *San Carlos Mission Church, about 1883.*
Johnson, photo.

PLATE 12.   *San Carlos Mission Church, After the Restoration of 1884.*
Johnson, photo.

More thorough work in photographing the missions was done by C. E. Watkins in the late seventies and early eighties. Eduard Vischer, a contemporary critic, says of his views:

"His fine conception and splendid effects deserve the highest encomium. . . . Could views of similar merit and effects have been taken in early times of all the missions as they stood within our recollection, such undertaking, now greatly interferred with by decay as well as many renovations, would have been of inestimable value to the historian or antiquary."

Mission Restoration. No account of the history of San Carlos Mission would be complete that did not consider the various attempts at repair and restoration, some of which has greatly modified the form and appearance of the mission church.

The first recorded action of this character was made by Father Sorentine, the parish priest, in March, 1856. At this time little or no attempt was made to repair or restore the ruined buildings, but only to locate the body of Father Serra among the ruins of the stone church. In writing the results of this investigation, Father Sorentine says:[42]

"The next day, the 11th [of March], the dirt that was in the altar fell on the gospel side and following the traditional directions, we began to excavate and we found in this one a well sealed vault, with a coffin, in which there was a priest with a stole and good vestments. We could see by the stole that it had epaulettes of fine gold, easily recognized. This body of a priest that we found, so luxuriously vested, something that none of the others had, makes me believe that it is one we are looking for."

But little was done until about 1884 when a new interest in the mission was aroused by the opening of the resort at Del Monte. Mrs. Leland Stanford and others became interested in the ruined mission and plans were made to render the church once again suitable for worship. By this time practically the entire roof had fallen in and many of the walls, especially those at the south corner, had crumbled and fallen. As the result of this endeavor, the church was once again habilitated, the walls being rebuilt and a new roof placed upon it.

Unfortunately, however, at this time repair was considered more important than restoration, the result being a repaired church which artistically was far inferior to the original structure. The chief and outstanding fault was that the new roof line was twelve or more feet higher than the older one and consequently at a much greater pitch. The former tile roof was low and with its gentle slope gave the church an appearance of greater length and beauty. The new roof with its exaggerated prominence gives

---

[42]*Letter of Cayetano Sorentine to Bishop Amat,* Monterey, March 12, 1856, in the Delfina de la Guerra Collection, Santa Barbara. Translated by Miss de la Guerra.

the towers a squatty appearance unknown to the padres, and otherwise
entirely changes the appearance of the church.   This was to some extent
made necessary by the substitution of shingles for the old tile roofing,
although it is probable that even with this in mind the original line could
have been more closely followed.   No attempt was made at that time to
restore any of the outlying buildings which composed the quadrangle.

ARCHITECTURAL FEATURES

ARCHITECTURAL FEATURES

The First Structures, 1771-1773. The first buildings constructed on the Carmel site were made of wood, easily obtained in abundance from the nearby forest of pines. Both Palou in his *Noticias* and Serra in his report of 1773 describe these temporary buildings and the rude stockade, which during the earlier years served as an additional protection against pilfering and possible hostile attacks of the natives.

This stockade, which Serra says was something more than seventy varas long by forty-three wide, was made of rough palings. It enclosed most of the mission buildings but not all of them, for the soldiers' barracks were just outside. In a prominent place was the cross and near at hand the hut of Father Serra and another crude structure which served in part as the provisional church. Palou says further that this chapel was one of six rooms in a house fifty by seven varas in size, four of the rooms being used as living quarters and another as a store room or granary. These were all built of wood and had flat mud roofs. That they were not permanent buildings may be judged from the nature of the material of which they were constructed, as well as by the fact that they were erected in such a very short time when laborers were scarce. Palou mentions only twelve men as working with Father Serra.[43]

Other Buildings, 1774. Several other buildings were constructed during 1774. As they were built partially of adobe it is probable that they were more permanent in character. Serra mentions five buildings about thirty by seven varas in size, as being constructed that year. One of these served as a work shop, two were for married servants, one was for the surgeon and another for the smith. Another wooden building with thatch roof was built for the captain of the guard. The record does not say that these buildings were within, or a part of, the enclosure mentioned the year before, and from the fact that no enclosure is mentioned thereafter until the completion of the later court in 1815, it is very probable that with the construction of more secure buildings the temporary stockade had been abandoned. These buildings were grouped around the open space spoken of as the mission plaza. The location of these early buildings in relationship to the later court and ruins now extant must be largely a matter of conjecture.[44]

The Adobe Church. It is regretted that reports are not available for the twenty years following 1774, the only evidence at hand being passing references found in the account of the death and burial of Father Serra in 1784, and at the time of the visit of Lapérouse in 1786. From these we gather that Serra was then living in a small room or cell made of adobe, which was

---

[43]See historical statement, *ante,* 18.

[44]For their conjectural location and form see plate 44.

a part of and closely connected with several other rooms; that the church was about one hundred varas from Serra's cell; and that the former was of considerable size since it could accommodate nearly all of the six hundred people present at Serra's funeral. This church had a place for the choir, a side room used as a sacristy, and there were several stations of the cross within the church. Lapérouse in 1786 speaks of this church as being "very neat, although covered with straw," and says that the president of the mission met him at the church door and conducted him to the foot of the "high altar."[45]

From these passages it is certain that the church of 1784 and 1786 was not the same as the temporary structure of 1773 and of course it cannot be the same as the present stone church which was not begun until 1793. There must therefore have been a church erected sometime previous to 1784 of which the records do not make satisfactory statement. Lack of direct evidence makes it very difficult to speak definitely regarding the nature or location of this second church. Many indications however point to its being located upon the site of the present building and that the position of the altar was identical with that of the present altar. If we may assume, as many things indicate, that Serra's room was located at or near the spot now marked by tradition as his death chamber, we have some basis by which to guide us in locating this church. Lapérouse in 1786 says the missionaries' house at that time was in front of the church, and Palou furnished the information that the distance Serra walked from his cell to the altar was "more than one hundred varas."[46] The location of the present church satisfies very well both of these conditions. Furthermore the absence of any record of the removal of bodies of Fathers Crespi and Serra, who were known to be buried in the older church, tends to confirm the belief that such was not necessary because of the fact that the new structure was erected upon ground already made holy not only by the ministration of these men but also as the resting place of their remains, and that the altar of the new was upon the site of the altar of the old church. Upon this point Father J. Adam says:

"Before concluding, it may be proper to answer the question as to what became of that church of stone, of which Fr. Junípero spoke when, just before dying, he requested Fr. Palou to lay his body close by that of Fr. Crespi, remarking: 'When they build the church of stone, let them throw me where they like.' Can we for a moment suspect that his religious friends had so little respect for his memory as to let him be buried outside of the consecrated ground? By no means. Why, then, is no notice taken of the removal of the remains of Fr. Crespi and Fr. Junípero from the old church to the new one? It is the general opinion of the old residents of Monterey that the new stone church, alluded to by Father Junípero, was built on the same spot where the old edifice stood, and according to this supposition the graves of the two first missionaries remained undisturbed and enclosed within the sanctuary of the new church, on the gospel side, as they were in the temporary building."[47]

[45]Serra's quarters are described as "su quartito ó celda que tenia de adoves." Palou, *Vida*, 270. For other references see Historical Narrative, *ante*, 21-22.

[46]Two hundred seventy-eight feet.

[47]Adams translation of Palou, *Life of Serra*, 149.

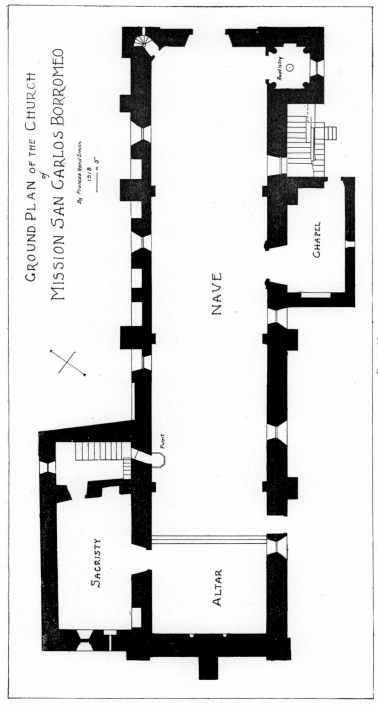

GROUND PLAN OF THE CHURCH
of
MISSION SAN CARLOS BORROMEO

By Frances Rand Smith.
1918

NAVE

SACRISTY

ALTAR

Pulpit

CHAPEL

Baptistry

PLATE 13.

47

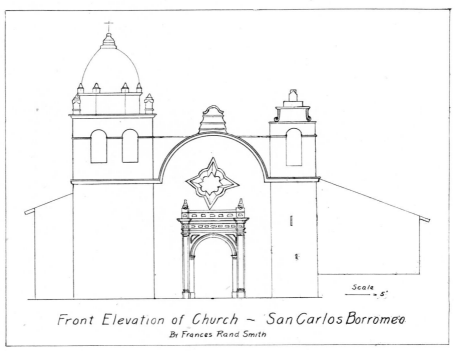

Front Elevation of Church ~ San Carlos Borromeo
By Frances Rand Smith

Scale = 5'

PLATE 14.

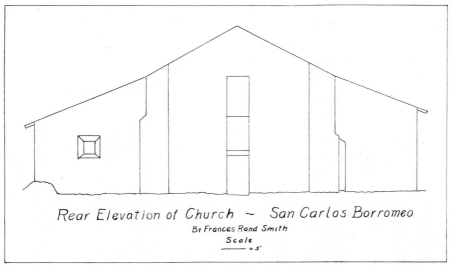

Rear Elevation of Church ~ San Carlos Borromeo
By Frances Rand Smith

Scale = 5'

PLATE 15.

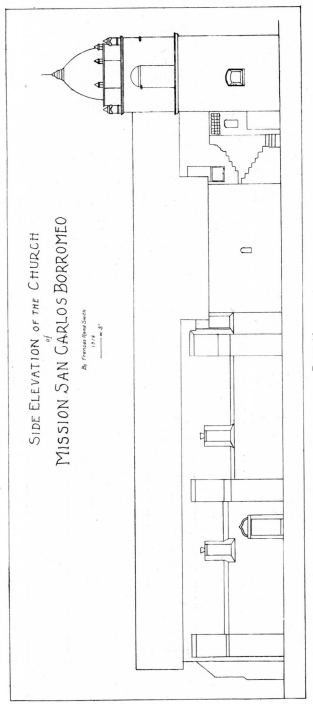

SIDE ELEVATION OF THE CHURCH
of
MISSION SAN CARLOS BORROMEO

By Francis Rand Smith
1918 —— = 5'

PLATE 16.

49

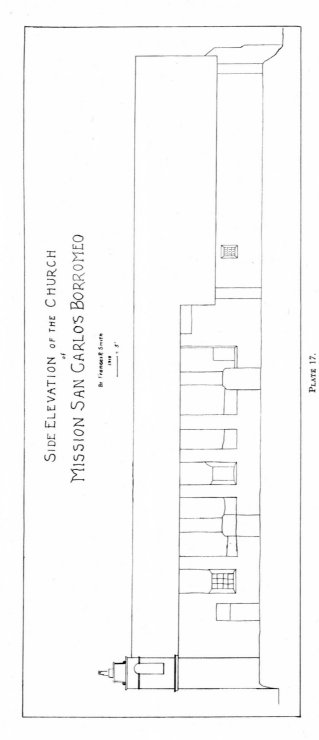

SIDE ELEVATION of the CHURCH
of
MISSION SAN CARLOS BORROMEO

By Francis R Smith
1918
——— = 5'

PLATE 17.

Using the Sykes sketch of 1794 as a basis for further deduction we must conclude that at least during the construction of the stone church, services were held elsewhere than upon the site just considered as that of the adobe church. It is however extremely probable that at that time a room of some existing building may have served this purpose as had been done during the earlier years. Vancouver in 1794 speaks of the stone church as in the process of construction but makes no mention of the place of worship used at that time. The cross shown upon the building to the left in the Sykes sketch would seem to indicate that for the time being it was used as the church (plate 2).

The Stone Church. Since the mission was primarily a religious institution it is customary to think of the church as the chief if not the only building connected with the establishment. Because also of the fact that at many mission sites the church alone now stands amidst the falling ruins of outbuildings it has to many minds come to be the belief that the church or chapel was the mission. This is untrue to fact. The church was the center of the religious life and around this the whole of the mission activities revolved but it did not alone constitute the mission, for in the days of the Spanish padres church, school, living quarters, workshops, granaries, fields and flocks each occupied an essential part in the make up of a typical California mission. Chief among these buildings was naturally the mission chapel or church.

As has been noted in a preceding paragraph the present church is the third to be built at Carmel. It measures one hundred sixty-seven feet four inches in total length and varies in width from fifty feet four inches at the north end to sixty-two feet at the sanctuary end, the difference in width being due to the baptistry and the sacristy respectively. The church proper is thirty-nine feet wide. The main walls are approximately five feet in thickness. It is constructed of sandstone, obtained near at hand.

As previously stated the present appearance of the church dates from 1884 when an effort was made under Father Casanova to restore it so that religious services could be resumed. A radical modification was made at this time, due to an attempt to give the roof a steeper incline, since shingles were to be substituted for roofing tiles. To accomplish this the peak of the roof was raised some twelve feet, while on the other hand the eaves over the chapel were lowered. The result of all this is to give the roof a prominence never dreamed of by the original builders.

The accompanying elevations show the roof lines and walls as they stood before these changes were made, and when the church had the appearance of greater length and dignity. In this construction was a fitness of proportion characteristic of Spanish architecture. By the use of photographs and traces left upon the building itself many of these points have been determined with a very marked degree of certainty. Through these various means the original height of the roof has been fixed at thirty-seven feet at its peak, and twenty-six feet at the eaves.

When built at these dimensions the main tower stood twenty-six feet above the peak of the roof and the cross even higher, while the smaller tower exceeded the height of the roof by nine feet. Six bells hung in these towers as late as 1852.[48] The larger tower is reached by an outside stairway, and is capped with a hollow dome of stone masonry, to which an entrance could be had from the northwest side (plate 9). There was originally an exterior entrance into the balcony through the larger belfry tower, the ceiled passage way being still noticeable.

Interior of the Church. The interior of the church of San Carlos Borromeo is one of the most picturesque of all the missions of California. The main chapel is twenty-eight feet eight and one-half inches in width and measures one hundred twenty-five feet four inches from the front wall to the first step approaching the sanctuary, from this point to the rear wall there is an additional twenty-five feet ten and one-half inches. This area is separated from the remainder of the church by a low railing as well as being elevated several inches above the floor level.

Subdued light is permitted to penetrate the thick walls through comparatively narrow windows, three on the left of the entrance and four on the right. A most interesting star window over the front entrance furnishes additional light to the church through the balcony.

The beauty of the nave was enhanced by an arched ceiling, the massive tile roof being supported by arches constructed in a most skillful manner. This is shown by photographs taken during the time the mission was in ruins. Of particular value upon this point is the photograph of the interior published by W. Clarence Brown (plate 19). This photograph is remarkable because it includes two of the three stone arches before their destruction, and it is particularly valuable in that it represents the best and most intricate construction in the church. Only at Carmel were stone arches extensively employed. As seen in the photograph the spring of the arch began on a line corresponding to the base of the windows, the curve being gradually met in the massive walls and stone pilasters (plates 19, 20, 21). From the line of the richly ornamented cornice the arch was built strictly for utility and it was the contact with the stone pilasters, the increased proportion of the upper wall, and the buttress against the same section (plate 13) which gave the line of thrust its resistance. In plate 20 the curve is drawn with the original contour showing the slight arch of the three sections. This construction has been referred to as a nave roof of vaulted and ancient con-

---

[48]See note 36, page 34. Two of these were added in 1820, see note 24, page 31. There were in all twenty-four bells located around the mission court. "el numero de las campanas colocadas en distintos puntos del cerco de esa mision, ascendia a veinte y cuatro." Vallejo, *Historia de California,* I, 67-8.

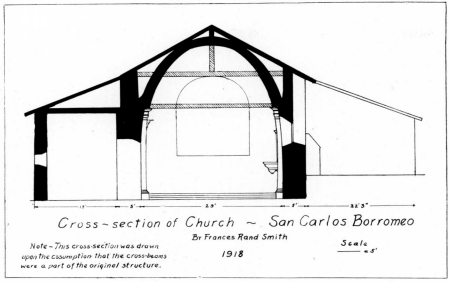

Cross~section of Church ~ San Carlos Borromeo

By Frances Rand Smith

1918

Note – *This cross-section was drawn upon the assumption that the cross-beams were a part of the original structure.*

Scale
= 5'

17'   5'   23'   5'   22'3"

PLATE 18.

PLATE 19. *Ruined Interior of Church.*
Brown, photo.

53

PLATE 21. *Ruins of Interior before 1880.* Perkins photo.

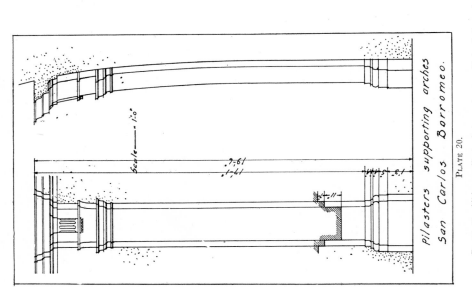

Pilasters supporting arches
San Carlos Borromeo.

Scale———1:0"

PLATE 20.

PLATE 21.—This excellent photograph was obtained through the kindness of the family of Mr. Perkins. The original plate with many others is now in the State Library. The most striking feature is the excellent reproduction of one of the three stone arches. The notched rafters are shown resting upon the supporting arch. The star window with its unique irregularity is plainly shown, as is also the stone arch supporting the balcony. In the foreground to the left is to be seen the remains of the stone pulpit and at the extreme left a niche in the wall which did not find a place in the restored church. The original floor tiles had not then been disturbed.

54

PLATE 23. *Star Window.*

Note the irregular form of the window, which is here correctly reproduced.

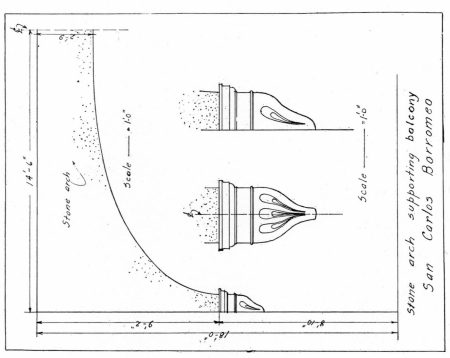

Stone arch supporting balcony
San Carlos Borromeo

PLATE 22.

55

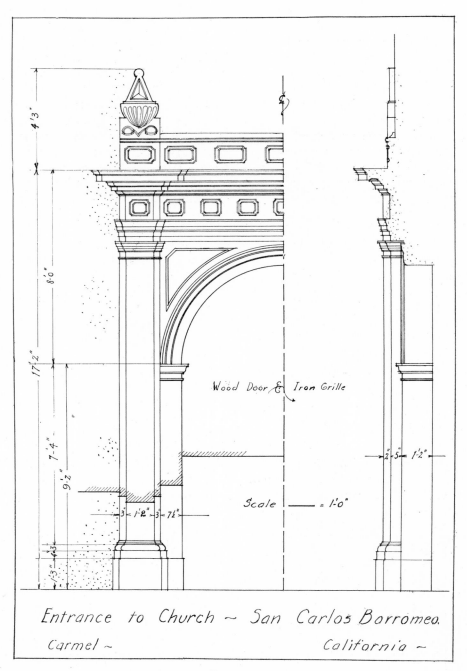

4'3"

17'2"

8'0"

7'4"

9'2"

1'3"

4'3

3 1'2 3 7½

Wood Door & Iron Grille

Scale ⎯⎯⎯⎯ = 1'0"

2 5 1'2"

Entrance to Church ~ San Carlos Borromeo.

Carmel ~   California ~

PLATE 24.

56

struction.[49] So unusual is the construction that it is quite possible the principle of the catenary curve may have been used in these arches.

In addition to the three stone arches supplemental wooden arches also helped to sustain the roof. Caps, which are still a part of the interior stone cornice, mark, it is said, the places upon which these wooden arches rested. One stone arch has remained and is quite as perfect as the day it was constructed. Although there is but little spring, it supports the spacious balcony. In the photographs it appears to be spanning the main entrance.

Upon entering the great doorway (plate 24), one may turn to the right and find a steep and narrow stairway. Twenty irregular sandstone steps, measuring about two feet six inches in length, one foot two inches in width, and with a nine inch rise, make two complete turns around a column of stone nine inches in diameter. These steps, worn by the tramp of Indian, priest and tourist, lead to the balcony, which is lighted by the famous star window. (Plate 23.)

The baptistry to the left of the entrance is a memento of workmen skilled in stone-cutting. For it should be stated that the numerous carvings in the soft sandstone used throughout the great walls of the church, form one of its most interesting features, the granite foundations upon which the edifice is built having provided resistance against earthquake and storm. Four columns support a Gothic ceiling, the ribs of which are carefully proportioned and are constructed of short lengths of sandstone. The floor of the baptistry is paved with tiles. The entrance is an arched doorway of stone (plate 25). A framework of wood fitted within the stone arch held perpendicular rods which formed an open screen.[50]

The chapel located at the left adjoining the baptistry is reached by the most elaborate doorway in the church (plate 26). Although the room measures twenty-eight feet by fourteen feet in size it is lighted by one small window whose outer curves are simple and effective. These outer lines appear to have represented a halo and the window probably held a small statue (plate 28). Upon the wall of this chapel is a colored decoration including a prayer in Spanish. This chapel may also be entered by means of an outside door.[51]

As one approaches further toward the altar another door is found leading to the left into the mission court. This is also shown in many of the photographs giving an exterior view of the church. It will be noticed that in the photographs by Johnson and others taken before 1884 that with the exception of the arched top, the doorway is without ornamentation. During the rebuilding the arched top was made square and it is said that the sandstone carvings from the doorway of the priest's quarters, then in ruin, were

[49]Benton, *The California Mission and its influence upon Pacific Coast Architecture,* in West Coast Magazine, Vol. IX, May, 1911, No. 2. See also Judson, *"The Architecture of the Missions,"* in Annual Publication of the Historical Society of Southern California, VII (1907-08), 116.

[50]Unfortunately the original baptismal font was badly damaged by vandals. *Father Sorentine to Bishop Amat,* March 12, 1856. *Ante,* note 42. It was later taken to Santa Cruz but subsequently returned to San Carlos.

[51]Paintings in this room were seen as late as 1837. *Ante,* note 33. This has been referred to as the chapel of the Crucifixion, *San Francisco Call* Aug. 29, 1884, and may have been the Chapel of the Pasion del Señor, built in 1818. *Ante,* note 23.

transferred and inserted within this doorway of the church (plates 30 and 31).

The altar of the church is approached by steps of excellent proportion which extend the width of the building, while a spacious arch in the rear wall gives added dignity. A plaque found in the debris of the altar (plate 32) was presented to Mrs. Leland Stanford by Father Casanova and is now in the collection of mission relics in the museum of Stanford University. This is outlined in gold paper and a circle of red pigment, probably ochre. The wood carving shown in plate 33 is a part of the same collection. To the right within the railing is the doorway to the sacristy (plate 34). The irregular shape of certain walls of the sacristy makes it quite probable that this part belonged to a group of buildings erected previous to the building of the stone church. It may have been the one shown in the sketch by Sykes in 1794.

In the sacristy is to be seen one of the well built stairways of the mission. This stairway is the approach to the pulpit, the floor of which is a solid piece of sandstone carving. The door of the pulpit is hand carved and is the same in design as that in the main doorway at San Fernando. It is probable that the designer at San Carlos worked also at San Fernando. The lavabo in the sacristy ranks as one of the finest examples of stone carving in the mission (plate 35).

The Mission Quadrangle. The records do not specify when the buildings composing the quadrangle were erected except that the report of 1815 says that the court was entirely enclosed by the construction of fifty varas of buildings during the preceding year.[52] It is probable that with the building of the stone church the center of mission life was shifted from the early plaza shown by Sykes to the area now seen to have been the mission enclosure.

The exterior limits of this quadrangle as shown in the ground plan herewith produced (plate 45) are based upon actual survey of the extant ruins supplemented by the plat and field notes of the United States engineer who made the survey when the lands were patented to the church. This survey was made by J. E. Terrell in December, 1858, and may be considered as representing the outline of the buildings and ruins as they stood at that date. Unfortunately it is not possible to identify accurately all of the corners in reference to buildings existing at present. It may be probable that the mission was then in such a state of dilapidation that it was impossible for the surveyor to determine the original purpose and relationship of the existing ruins. It is, therefore, to be expected that present ruins may not in all cases be capable of identification upon the surveyor's plat and that in places the survey may not properly represent the external lines of the court. The most noticeable feature to be seen in studying this plat is that the court does not constitute a true rectangle, but was probably built to conform to ground levels.

---

[52]*Ante,* note 22. See plate 44 for conjectural location of these buildings.

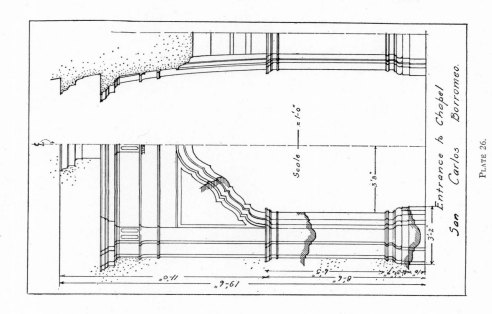

Entrance to Chapel

San Carlos Borromeo.

PLATE 26.

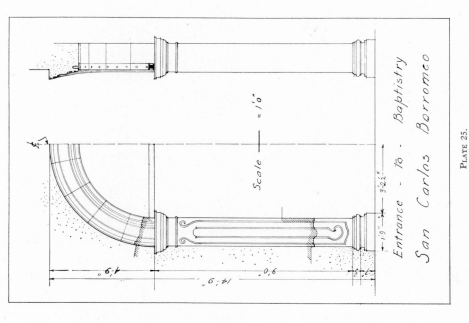

Entrance - To - Baptistry

San Carlos Borromeo

PLATE 25.

PLATE 28. *Chapel Window.* Slevin, photo.

PLATE 27. *Baptistry Window.* Slevin, photo.

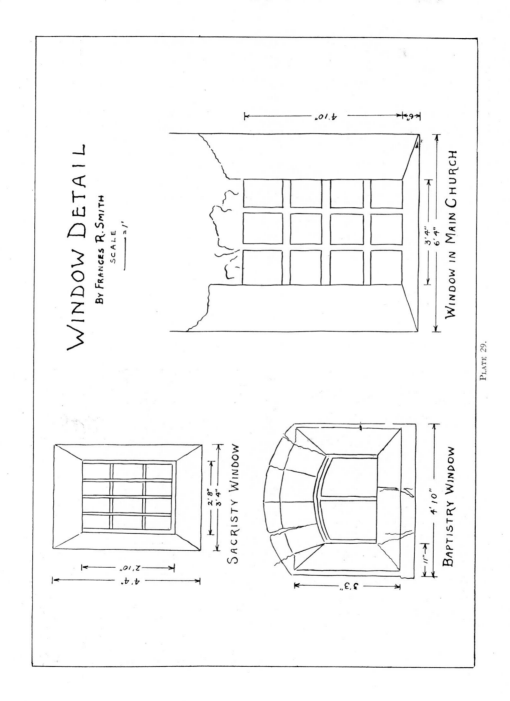

WINDOW DETAIL

By Frances R. Smith

SCALE ____ = 1'

Window in Main Church

4' 10"

6' 9"

3' 4"
6' 4"

Sacristy Window

2' 8"
3' 4"

2' 10"
4' 4"

Baptistry Window

4' 10"

11"

3' 3"

Plate 29.

61

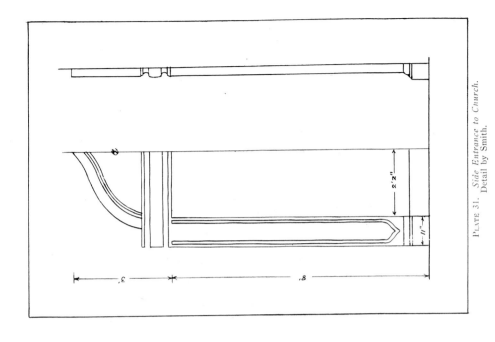

PLATE 31. *Side Entrance to Church.*
Detail by Smith.

PLATE 30. *Side Entrance to Church.*
Slevin, photo.

PLATE 33. *Wood Carving Used in Interior Decoration.*
Stanford Museum.

PLATE 32. *Plaque Found Near Altar of Church.*
Stanford Museum.

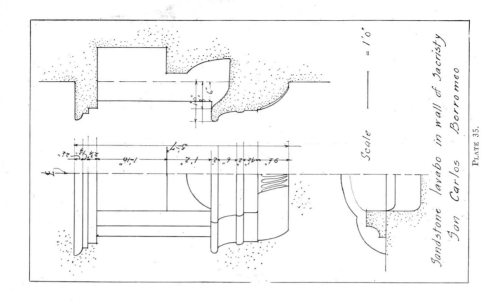

Scale ———— = 1'0"

Sandstone lavabo in wall of Sacristy
San Carlos Borromeo

PLATE 35.

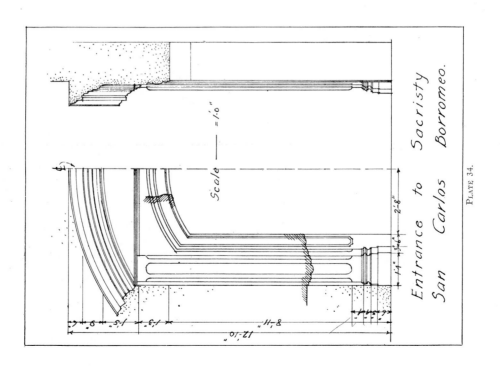

Scale ———— = 1'0"

Entrance to Sacristy
San Carlos Borromeo.

PLATE 34.

Adjoining the church upon its front and eastern corner stood the buildings which began, or rather, continued the enclosure. A recent survey confirms the United States plat when it indicates that they did not join the front of the church at right angles but at an angle of eighty-seven and one-half degrees.[53] That these buildings joined upon the front of the church there can be no question, although at present there are no adobe remains within approximately forty feet of the church, this space having been used for many years as a driveway.

The evidence supporting the claim that the ruins connected with the church is as follows: In the first place, it is stated in the mission report of 1815 that the quadrangle was enclosed and various descriptions after that date mention definitely this enclosure; second, photographs by Muybridge and Johnson show very plainly a wall extending northward from the church for a distance not less than twenty-five feet, while numerous other photographs taken before the restoration of the church show markings upon the facade of the church such as would be made only by adjoining buildings, which had but recently fallen away or had been removed;[54] and third, the remaining adobe ruins and stone foundations indicate a continuation of the buildings which, if extended, would join the church in such manner as to explain the markings in the photographs referred to.

From the data at hand the first section has been restored. The side walls are formed by continuing existing ruined walls. The end is determined from certain foundation stones to be found extending eastward from the corner of the church. This portion was probably used by the mission priests as living quarters, as indicated in the accounts of Lapérouse in 1786 and Du Petit-Thouars in 1837, as well as by present day tradition. On the other hand, an examination of the Sykes sketch made at the time of Vancouver's visit shows upon the right and in front of the stone church, then being constructed, a long building surmounted by a cross, thus indicating that it may then have been the temporary mission church.

The buildings nearer the northern corner of the court are fortunately in a better state of preservation. Existing adobe ruins laid bare by excavations under Father R. M. Mestres show plainly the postion and thickness of these walls (plates 36-40). That this portion of the building at least was more than one story in height is indicated by a Muybridge photograph (plate 7). In it are to be seen the elevation of the wall above the top of the door with projecting floor beams and windows for the upper floor. It is probable that the upper story was a loft which covered the whole of this range of buildings.

The ground plans for the buildings along the northeastern side of the court were worked out from existing ruins, photographic evidence, and from other data gathered several years ago. In the corner is one large room.[55]

---

[53] See note 37.

[54] See any front view of church about 1880 or before.

[55] The author saw this as one large room in 1908 before the excavation made for road work had removed a portion of the above ruins.

Adjoining this room to the east are the adobe remains of three smaller ones. These rooms are about sixteen feet wide inside measurement, and measure respectively twenty-nine, sixteen and eight feet in length.

These three rooms are six feet narrower than the corner room previously described, the extra space being occupied by a portico of that width as shown in the sketch of Wm. Smythe (plate 3). An excellent photograph by Fiske clearly shows that of these three rooms the larger one alone had a door or other exterior opening (plate 41). It may be of interest to note that this door has a striking similarity to the one removed from the adobe ruins during the restoration of 1884, and placed at the side of the stone church.[56] The other openings from these rooms into the court are of necessity largely conjectural, as the ruined walls fail to give satisfactory evidence as to their existence and location.

In the restoration of the building adjoining those just described there is now but little to guide the investigator, for the ruined adobe walls which at one time continued the enclosure have now disappeared. However, knowing from the documents that the court here was enclosed by buildings, and acting upon data obtained in 1908, before these walls had been entirely obliterated to satisfy a temporary demand for road material, this portion has been reconstructed. Acting upon this data these buildings have been indicated as of the same width as the room at the northeast corner. That in their general form and size these buildings have been correctly outlined there seems to be but little ground for doubt.[57]

The United States survey plat shows an extension of nine feet along a portion of the northeast side of the court. Just what these lines represent is not determined in a fully satisfactory manner. It is probable, however, that they represent a projection such as a covered porch, as is suggested by the sketch of Wm. Smythe. Adjoining the corner of the court upon the east is a small rectangular space set off in such a manner as to indicate a building about twenty-six by nineteen feet in size. This was probably built in this manner to serve as a buttress to support the walls of the range of buildings just described, or it may have been a supplemental building added later.

From these buildings the court turned to the southwest at an angle of ninety and one-half degrees. The inner wall of this portion is clearly shown by existing ruins which extend for a distance of about one hundred fifty feet.[58] The outer wall of this portion of the quadrangle has disappeared, but that an adobe wall did exist is indicated by notations upon the plat of the

[56]A close examination of the Fiske photograph referred to shows very clearly the characteristics of this doorway. According to the statement of Father R. M. Mestres, this door of the church had been obtained from one of the adobe ruins. *Ante,* 57.

[57]The evidence favoring this conclusion is as follows: First, the line of the United States survey indicates that the buildings here were wider than those previously described, rather than narrower. Second, notwithstanding the many points of conflict between the sketch of San Carlos in 1823 (plate 3), and the archeological evidence now at hand, the former does support strongly the idea of continuous and more or less uniform buildings. This also is borne out in the restoration of Oriana Day (plate 8), which, however, without further evidence, does not stand as an independent source. Third, the Fiske photograph of 1880 (plate 41), shows walls which have now disappeared. Unfortunately, however, from the picture it is impossible to determine definitely the position of these walls with reference to their distance from the court.

[58]The first 30 feet have disappeared, this being used as a roadway.

PLATE 36. *Mound of Ruins, January, 1920.*
Coy, photo.

PLATE 37. *Same Mound After Excavation, April, 1921.*
Coy, photo.

Plate 38.

Plate 40.

Plate 39.

Excavated Ruins, April, 1921. Coy, photo.

PLATE 41. *Ruins of San Carlos Mission about 1880.*   Photo by Fiske.

This is one of the most valuable photographs here presented, as it shows the whole sweep of mission ruins as they were about 1880. Much of the northeast side of the mission court is well preserved in this photograph. In the foreground is shown what, according to Mr. Muchado, for many years caretaker of the mission, was the foundation of the herder's cabin. We must agree that it was an excellent position as it commanded a view of the valley for many miles. This illustration is reproduced from the collection of Mr. Chas. B. Turrill.

PLATE 42. *Ruins of Mission Quadrangle, January, 1921.*
Slevin, photo.

PLATE 43. *Ruins of Mission Quadrangle, 1908.*
Slevin, photo.

United States surveyor. Its foundations therefore will probably be revealed by future excavations. The windows and doors leading into the court have been restored in the ground plan approximately as shown in these ruins.

At the end of the one hundred fifty feet just described the ruined adobe wall terminates in a well-defined corner, thus indicating the end of a building. Acting upon the following statement by Ruschenberger that there was an entrance to the court on this side, a wagon entrance has been indicated in the ground plan at this point. He says:[59]

"The mission building is, perhaps, a hundred yards square, one story high, and roofed with tiles. We rode through the gate, which was just ready to fall from its hinges, into the great central court, round which it is built, where we found eight or ten Indians engaged in repairing the roof."

In reference to the remainder of the quadrangle there is little evidence now to be found. It is probable that this portion of the quadrangle was constructed in a less substantial manner than the other parts. That the exterior walls were built of adobe is indicated upon the surveyor's plat,[60] but time has obliterated all surface traces of them as well as of the inner walls. It is extremely probable that excavations now in progress will show the exact location of all these walls.

That there were buildings enclosing the whole area of the mission court, however, is well established from documentary sources, and subsoil excavations have brought to light much corroborative data. In the annual report for the year 1815 it is stated that during the year there had been erected several buildings necessary to enclose the court.[61] Ruschenberger in 1836 describes the mission as built around a great central court. Du Petit-Thouars, who visited the mission in 1837, states in his description that the court was enclosed on all four sides by buildings.[62] In addition to these statements there is the sketch of the rear of the mission in 1839 reproduced by Laplace,[63] which shows the greater portion to have been enclosed by buildings, although it is impossible to determine much regarding their form or the material of which they were constructed. It is not improbable that buildings of light adobe had been erected along these two sides of the court either for workshops or neophytes' dwellings. All the walls have now disappeared but at the time of the survey of 1858 the outer and stronger wall of the adobe still remained, although even then in a ruined form.

As the side of the court approaches the church it is noted that the outer wall does not connect with the rear wall of the stone church, but lies some fifteen or more feet to the rear. Furthermore the surveyor's plat seems to show a projection of the church into the rear. When comparison is made with the sketch reproduced by Laplace these irregularities are explained,[64]

[59]Ruschenberger, *Narrative*, 507.
[60]Notations on the plat definitely state that the wall on the southeast side was an adobe. The other is merely described as an "old wall."
[61]*Archivo Misiones, Papeles Originales*, I, 372.
[62]Du Petit-Thouars, *Voyage*, II, 116.
[63]Laplace, *Campagne*, VI, 294 (plate 4).
[64]Plate 4.

for it is seen in the drawing that unless the laws of perspective were entirely disregarded the artist did not intend to show the rear wall of the court as joining directly upon the corner of the church, but rather several feet to the rear. The sketch then shows a lean-to building adjoining the rear of the church. There was probably a door at the corner of the court between the rear wall and the church through which access was had to this outbuilding.[65] From the representation of a corral around this structure it seems that it may have served in 1839 at least as a shelter for the milch cows.

That there were numerous other buildings serving the purpose of the mission outside of the enclosure just described is indicated by the various reports and sketches which have come down from the earlier period. The Smythe sketch of 1823 shows several buildings located outside, in addition to the rude huts of the Indians. Excavations among the ruins surrounding the mission enclosure may disclose the location and form of many of these buildings, but at present there is but little to indicate their number or location. It has been thought best, therefore, to include in this study only those buildings which were a part of, or definitely attached to, the mission court.[66]

The Mission Bells. No description of San Carlos would be complete without reference to its bells, for the bells played an important part in the life of every Spanish mission. They made known the hour of rising and the time of morning worship. At their sound the neophytes went forth to toil and were summoned to food and rest. The bells pealed forth glad welcome to arriving friends and tolled their dolorous lamentation at the death of members of the mission family.

Around the court at San Carlos hung some twenty-four bells of various sizes. At least six of these hung in the two towers of the church. Two of the larger bells were added during the year 1820. Unfortunately the only bell which has remained continuously at the mission has been recast during recent years, and but little is known regarding the history or present location of the other original bells. It is not improbable, however, that further research will disclose many facts still unknown and may make possible the identification of some of the bells which have drifted away from their proper surroundings.[67]

The Burial Ground. On the side of the church opposite the court lies the cemetery. All agree as to its position, but there is as yet no certainty as to its exact extent. This is due to the fact that a well defined wall divided the area described by various authorities as a cemetery into two distinct parts.[68] The wider area is shown upon the plat of the survey of 1858 and would allow for the burial ground space approximately one

---

[65]Vischer represents the walls of the buildings as being very massively built.

[66]For conjectural location of some of these buildings, see plate 44.

[67]For references regarding the bells, see notes 24, 36 and 48. A most valuable study of mission campanology is now being made by Mrs. Alice Harriman of Los Angeles.

[68]This wall is clearly shown in the photographs reproduced herewith. (Plates 5, 9 and 10.)

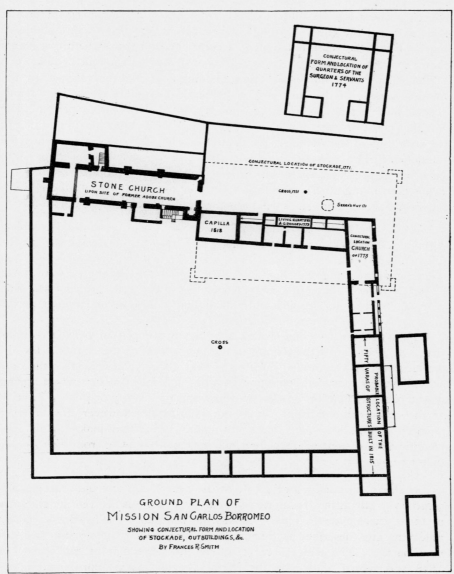

CONJECTURAL
FORM AND LOCATION OF
QUARTERS OF THE
SURGEON & SERVANTS
1774

CONJECTURAL LOCATION OF STOCKADE, 1771.

STONE CHURCH
UPON SITE OF FORMER ADOBE CHURCH

CROSS, 1771

SERRA'S HUT (?)

CAPILLA
1818

LIVING QUARTERS
& GRANARY, 1773

CONJECTURAL
LOCATION
CHURCH
OF 1773

CROSS

FIFTY VARAS OF

PROBABLE LOCATION OF

STRUCTURES BUILT IN 1815

GROUND PLAN OF
MISSION SAN CARLOS BORROMEO
SHOWING CONJECTURAL FORM AND LOCATION
OF STOCKADE, OUTBUILDINGS, &c.
BY FRANCES R. SMITH

PLATE 44.

hundred sixty in length by slightly less than sixty feet in average width. The smaller space lies near the church and is about one hundred long by twenty feet wide. That this latter was the burial ground seems indicated by the Smythe sketch of 1823, as well as that of Laplace of 1839. That this smaller space was inadequate for this purpose would appear very reasonable, but why a substantial wall should divide the grounds is an unsolved question unless the original burial ground had been enlarged, the wall being allowed to remain. Of the existence of this wall there can be no doubt. It is very distinctly reproduced in the Fiske photograph of the ruins of the Mission Church (plate 10), which shows the rear portion of the wall still standing up to a level with the eaves of the sacristy, a height of twelve feet. It is also clearly indicated in the "Alemany Plat," 1854. (Plate 5.)

According to tradition, an unmarked grave is situated in front of the mission church for the bandit Garcia, a member of the band under the leadership of Vasquez, who asked in his deathbed repentance, it is said, that he be buried where the worshipers of the mission might ever tread upon his grave. Before the great door of the church is another grave, that of the weary and worn little Costanoan Indian. This honor was earned when, during the strength of her young womanhood, she helped to bear the burdens in the building of San Carlos.

In the shelter of the great stone walls of the mission of San Carlos Borromeo itself is the last resting place of the priests and Indians who were the builders of the mission. Here, too, rest Serra and Crespi, who conceived the plan of the stone church, and Lasuén, who erected it. Thus, of the little band of four associates, in the convent school of Majorca (*Spanish,* Mallorca), in the Balearic Isles, Serra, Palou, Verger, and Crespi, who in later life set out together on their high-souled missionary adventure to the New World, and all four of whom cooperated to the end in the work of building up the superb chain of California missions, it came to pass that two still sleep side by side.

To the architectural beauty of the ruin at Carmel, the spot where Father Junípero labored and died, Helen Hunt Jackson pays this tribute:[69]

"His grave is under the ruins of the beautiful stone church of his mission,—the church which he saw only in ardent and longing fancy. It was perhaps the most beautiful, though not the grandest of the mission churches; and its ruins have today a charm far exceeding all the others. The fine yellow tint of the stone, the grand and unique contour of the arches, the beautiful star-shaped window in the front, the simple yet effective lines of carving on pilaster and pillar and doorway, the symmetrical Moorish tower and dome, the worn steps leading up to the belfry,—all make a picture whose beauty, apart from hallowing associations, is enough to hold one spell-bound."

---

[69]Jackson, Helen Hunt, *Glimpses of California and the Missions,* 43.

BIBLIOGRAPHY

Printed Works

Adam, J.   See under Palou.

Bancroft, H. H., *History of California.*   San Francisco, 1884-1890.

Bartlett, J. R., *Personal narrative of explorations and incidents, . . . during the years 1850, '51, '52 and '53.*   New York, 1854.

Beechey, F. W., *Narrative of a voyage to the Pacific . . . in the years 1825, '26, '27, '28.*   Philadelphia, 1832.

Benton, Arthur B., *The California mission and its influence upon Pacific Coast architecture,* in the West Coast Magazine, X, 137-160 (May, 1911).

Cole, G. W., *Missions and mission pictures; a contribution towards an iconography of the Franciscan missions of California,* in California State Library, *News note,* V (1910), 390-412.

Duflot de Mofras, Eugène, *Exploration du territoire de l'Orégon des Californies . . . pendant les années 1840, 1841, et 1842.*   Paris, 1844.

Du Petit-Thouars, Abel, *Voyage autour du monde sur la frégate la Vénus pendant les années,* 1836-1839.   Paris, 1840.

Engelhardt, C. A. (*in religion* Zephyrin).   *The missions and missionaires of California.*   San Francisco, 1908-1916.

Hittell, T. H., *History of California.*   San Francisco, 1898.

Jackson, Helen Hunt, *Glimpses of California and the missions.*   Boston, 1902.

Judson, Wm. L., *Architecture of the missions,* in Historical Society of Southern California, *Annual Publications,* VII, 114-118.

Lapérouse, Jean Francois de Galaup, *Voyage de la Pérouse autour du Monde.*   Paris, 1798.

Laplace, [Cyrille Pierre Theodore], *Campagne de Circumnavigation de la frégate l'Artémise pendant les années 1837, 1838, 1839 et 1840.*   Paris, 1841-1854.

Palou, Francisco, *Noticias de la Nueva California.*   San Francisco, 1874.

Relacion historica de la vida y apostolicas tereas del Venerable Padre Fray Junípero Serra.   Mexico, 1787.

Francisco Palou's life . . . of the Venerable Father Junípero Serra.   Pasadena (G. W. James), 1913.

Life of Ven. Padre Junípero Serra. . . . Tr. by Very Rev. J. Adam.   San Francisco, 1884.

Richman, Irving B., *California under Spain and Mexico.*   New York, 1911.

Ruschenberger, Wm. S. W., *A voyage round the world . . . in 1835, 1836 and 1837.*   Philadelphia, 1838.

T. H. S.   *The death and burial of Father Junípero Serra,* in Hutching's Illustrated California Magazine, IV (1860), 493-496.

Vancouver, George, *A voyage of discovery . . . in the year 1790, 1791, 1792, 1793, 1794, and 1795.*   London, 1798.

Vischer, Eduard, *Missions of upper California, 1872.*   San Francisco, 1872.

Manuscript Material

(Chiefly in the Bancroft Collection)

Bancroft, H. H., *Personal Observations, 1874.*

De Croix to Fages, November 12, 1770, in *Archives of California, Provincial State Papers,* I, 69–71.

Fages to Palou, May 29, 1785, in *Archives of California, Provincial Records,* III, 50.

Informe de San Carlos, December 31, 1810, in *Archivo de las Misiones, Papeles Originales,* I, 328.

Informe de San Carlos, December 31, 1815, in *Archivo de las Misiones, Papeles Originales,* I, 372.

Informe de San Carlos, December 31, 1818, in *Archivo de las Misiones, Papeles Originales,* I, 432.

Informe de San Carlos, December 31, 1820, in *Archivo de las Misiones, Papeles Originales,* I, 328.

Informe de San Carlos, December 31, 1822, in *Archivo de las Misiones, Papeles Originales,* I, 554–556.

Lasuén to Arrillaga, June 7, 1794, in *Archivo del Arzobispado de San Francisco,* I, 38–39.

Lasuén to Borica, December 10, 1794, in *Archivo de la Mision de Santa Barbara, Papeles Miscelaneos,* VI, 219–220.

Lasuén, Estado general bienal 1793–4, Mar. 11, 1795, in *Archivo de la Mision de Santa Barbara, Informes y Correspondencia,* XII, 54–61.

Lasuén, Report, 1797–1798, in *Archivo de la Mision de Santa Barbara Papeles Miscelaneos,* XII, 65–68.

Lasuén, Representacion, November 12, 1800, in *Archivo de la Mision de Santa Barbara, Papeles Miscelaneos,* II, 154–240.

Notas, March 1, 1795, in *Archives of California, State Papers Missions,* II, 4–8.

Payeras, Report, December 31, 1818, in *Archivo de la Mision de Santa Barbara, Informes y Correspondencia,* XII, 451–455.

Payeras, Report, May 4, 1819, *Ibid,* 98–104.

Sal, Estado, December 31, 1797, in *Archives of California, State Papers Missions,* II, 120.

Serra, Representacion de 21 Mayo, 1773, in *Archives of California, Provincial State Papers,* I, 103–137, also in *Archivo de la Mision de Santa Barbara,* I, 83–118.

Serra, Informe, 1774, in *Archivo de la Mision de Santa Barbara, Informes y Correspondencia,* I, 146–154.

Sorentine to Bishop Amat, Monterey, March 12, 1856, in the *Delfine de la Guerra Collection,* Santa Barbara.

Vallejo, Mariano G., *Historia de California,* 5 volumes.

INDEX.

Gentile, Indians, 20.

Gothic ceiling in baptistry, 57.

Granary (1771), 19, 45; well filled (1794), 27.

Grinding flour, method of, 27.

Herder's cabin (plate 41), 69.

Hittell, cited, 31.

Indians, huts of thatch (1773), 20; village described by Lapérouse (1786), 22–23; by Vancouver (1794), 27; quarters of (1800), 28; numbers of, seven hundred and forty (1786), 23; eight hundred (1794), 27; five hundred (1834), 34; eight or ten Indians working (1836), 32; two or three families (1837), 33; not over thirty (1841), 34; tenantless (1852), 34; life of, daily routine, 23; food, 23; grinding meal, 27.

Inventory of property (1834), 32.

Irrigation, possible in Carmel Valley, 18.

Jackson, Helen Hunt, quoted, 74.

James, Geo. Wharton, cited, 17, 18, 24.

Johnson, C. W. J., photographer, 38, 65; photographs by, frontis, (plates 11, 12), 40.

Judson, W. L., cited, 57.

Kitchen (1771), 19.

Lapérouse, 45, 65; visits mission (1786), 22–23; picture, 33.

Laplace, at mission (1839), 34, 71; sketch of mission (plate 4), 29.

Lasuén, 74; president of missions, 22; builds stone church, 23–24; cited, 24; quoted, 28.

Lavabo in sacristy, 58; detail of (plate 35), 64.

Lime made of sea shells, 27.

Living quarters, 45; at the presidio (1770), 17; in 1771, 18–19; in 1837, 33.

Lower California Indians, 18.

Marines, help build mission, 18.

Mestres, Father R. M., 65, 66.

Mill, presented to mission (1786), 23.

Mofras. See Duflot.

Monterey Bay, Spanish occupation of, 17.

Mortar, and whitewash on walls, 31; of adobe, 38; made of shells, 27; wooden wall plastered over, 20.

Mount Calvary, 31.

Muchado (plate 41), 69.

Muybridge, E. J., photographer, 38, 65; photograph by (plate 7), 36.

Neophytes. See Indians.

Orchard. See Garden.

Organ, presented by Vancouver, 27; still in use (1837), 34.

Ovens, 21.

Palou, 21, 22, 45, 74; cited, 17, 18, 22, 24, 46.

Paintings, in church (1786), 22; in chapel (1837), 33, 57.

Patent issued to church (1859), 37.

Payeras quoted, 31.

Perkins, photographer, 38; photograph by (plate 21), 54.

Pilasters, 52; detail of (plate 20), 54.

Pines, 45.

Plaque (plate 32), 58.

Portolá, 17.

Presidio, 18, 24.

Provisional church, at Carmel (1771), 18; in 1773, 20; conjectural location (plate 44), 73. See also Church.

Pulpit, 58.

Punta de Pinos, 19.

Quadrangle, 58, 65–66, 71–72; enclosed (1815), 31, 58; buildings more than one story (plate 7), 36; described by Ruschenberger (1836), 32; described by Du Petit-Thouars (1837), 33.

Quarters. See Living quarters.

Ravelins, 20.

Removal of mission to Carmel, 17, 18, 19.

Repairs on mission (1824), 31.

Restoration of stone church (1884), 41–42; photographs (plates 11, 12), 40.

Richman, cited, 32.

Roof, flat on early building (1771), 19; flat of clay and mud (1773), 20, 45; of thatch (1774), 20, 21, 45; flat earth roof (1774), 21; church roof of straw (1786), 22, 46; stone church roof of tile, 24; arched roof, 34; roof partly fell (1852), 37; in ruins (1874), 37–38; roof removed, 38; shown in photographs (plates 9, 10), 39; height changed during restoration (1884), 41–42; original height determined, 52.

Ruíz, master mason, 24.

Ruschenberger, quoted, 32, 71.

Sacristy, 38, 58; entrance (plate 34), 64; window in (plate 29), 61; lavabo in (plate 35), 64; roof renewed, 39.

Sailors, cut timber, 19.

Sal, quoted, 24.

San Antonio de Padua founded, 18.

Sanctuary, 52.

San Fernando, Mission, carvings similar to, 58; College of, 17.

San Francisco Call, cited, 57.

San Francisco Mission, 24, 28.

San Luís Obispo Mission, 18.

Santa Clara Mission, 24, 27.

Secularization, 31–32.

Serra, 17, 18, 20, 21, 25; as church builder (note 17), 24; death and burial, 21–22; buried in adobe church, 46; remains, 38; hut of, 18, 45; conjectural location of (plate 44), 73; room or cell of, 45.

Servants' quarters (1774), 21.

Slevin, photographs by (plates 42, 43), 70.

Smith's quarters, 21.

Smythe, Wm., 66, 72; sketch by (plate 3), 29.

Soldiers, aid in building, 18, 19.

Soledad secularized, 34.

o